"This is showbiz from the very intimate inside. How inside? Leonard was literally the third person on Cary Grant's honeymoon with Dyan Cannon...and writes all about it! Forty years in the film publicity trenches. You'll read all about life in the movies in the more glorious and glamorous 70s, 80s, and 90s... Steve McQueen, Peter Sellers, Warren Beatty, Barbra Streisand and on and on and on. A thousand times more interesting and sophisticated than today's gossip mongers. Morpurgo was right in there organizing, advising, encouraging and taking the heat for the cream of the movie crop as well as the heads of state from around the world. You love movies?... Don't miss Of Kings and Queens and Movie Stars."

Sid Ganis, Producer and President of the Academy of Motion Picture Arts and Sciences.

"This is a fun and fantastic reading experience. Leonard Morpurgo has worked with the famous, and his frank and entertaining stories about them are eye-openers. It's an insider's look at Hollywood egos, past and present."

Henri Bollinger, founder, president of the Entertainment Publicists Professional Society and past president of the Publicists Guild of America.

"A truly gifted bard, Leonard Morpurgo proves once again that truth is indeed stranger than fiction --- even in Hollywood. Wonderfully entertaining and great reading."

David A. Weitzner, Director, Summer Program School of Cinematic Arts, University of Southern California

"An amusing and informative collection of stories about the author's adventures in the PR trade, told with an engagingly wry and self-deprecating good humor."

Michael York

"If you want to know what it is like to be a publicity pro from the days of Cary Grant to George Clooney this is a great read. It is interesting, funny and enlightening."

Robert J. Dowling, former editor-in-chief and publisher of The Hollywood Reporter.

OF KINGS AND QUEENS AND MOVIE STARS

by Leonard Morpurgo

OF KINGS AND QUEENS AND MOVIE STARS
Copyright © 2009 by Leonard Morpurgo.
All rights reserved.

Printed in the United States of America. No part of this book may be used or reproduced in any manner whatsoever without written permission except in the case of brief quotations embodied in critical articles or reviews.

For information contact:
Global Book Publishers
269 S. Beverly Drive, Suite 1442, Beverly Hills, CA 90212.
www.bookpubintl.com

OF KINGS AND QUEENS AND MOVIE STARS
ISBN: 978-0-9818222-3-5

Library of Congress Control Number: 2009924814

Typography & Cover: Kirk Thomas, www.kirks-graphics.com

For Elena-Beth, Thierry, Benjamin, Bridget and, of course, Violet.

CONTENTS

INTRODUCTION 1

HONEYMOONS 3

A ROYAL PAIN 13

EARLY DAYS 23

BULLIES 26

ROMANCE 33

MORE "LAWRENCE" 37

"OLIVER!" 41

PETERS 46

BARBRA 53

MOSCOW 56

SEX IN HAMBURG AND OTHER GERMAN DELIGHTS . 62

SPACESHIPS IN MEXICO 68

FABULOUS FULLER 78

SWEDEN AND OTHER PLACES 80

ON TARGET 83

CANNES CAN DO 93

CONTENTS

REVOLUTION!..................................110

AWAY FROM IT ALL............................113

WE SHOT J.R..................................116

TWILIGHT ZONE...............................121

BABES!......................................123

DINNER WITH SIDNEY..........................136

IT'S A JUNGLE OUT THERE.....................138

FIRSTS......................................140

NOW WE'RE COOKIN'...........................144

MUSIC TO MY EARS............................149

LEE MARVIN—AND OTHER BOOZERS................155

STEVE McQUEEN...............................162

DISASTERS AT DEAUVILLE AND MONACO...........167

COLD BLOOD..................................173

ODDS AND END................................176

FINAL WORDS.................................184

OF KINGS AND QUEENS AND MOVIE STARS

INTRODUCTION

For more than 40 years I've traveled the world as an international film publicist, acting as father confessor, whipping boy, friend—and sometimes enemy, to Hollywood celebrities.

Here are more than a hundred stories about those travels, some of them funny or whimsical, others tragic or sad. They will take the reader from Cannes to Tokyo, from a royal premiere in London to a film studio in Mexico, from the Alps to South America.

We're all part of the times we live in and so it was that I became caught in a failed revolution in France, a military dictatorship in Argentina and a cold war "international incident" in Moscow.

These stories have been packaged thematically, not chronologically. It was written this way because this is how I remembered. A story about the handling of a drunken Duke of Windsor would remind me of an embarrassing incident with the Queen of Belgium and another with the Queen of Holland. I was the third person on Cary Grant's honeymoon with Dyan Cannon, which leads to my own honeymoon with director Stanley Kramer—and without my wife.

Not all the celebrities and film executives in these stories have huge egos. Many are quiet and self-contained or vulnerable and afraid. Others are funny and gregarious. In other words, they're just people. True, they are people who live magnified lives and are used to having their every action scrutinized. Perhaps the best word to describe the majority of celebrities is "guarded".

Sometimes they would let that guard down, such as the time I accompanied Omar Sharif to a Hamburg brothel or listened to Lee Marvin make intimate confessions when he fell off the wagon.

This is written with a unique perspective on Hollywood. I've worked as an executive at two major studios—Columbia Pictures for nearly 11 years, where I was Director of European Publicity and Promotion, and Universal Studios for five minutes as head of International Advertising and

Publicity. I was at Lorimar when it was one of the mini-majors—before that generation of would-be studios over-extended and disappeared or were devoured by real studios, to be replaced by other ambitious independents with deep pockets. From there I moved across town to a television network, CBS, but had nothing to do with television. I was in the theatrical films division, which managed to lose more money in a couple of years than some nations do.

Included in my eclectic résumé are stints as vice president at three Hollywood public relations agencies. One was very small, only two of us during lean times. Rogers & Cowan on the other hand, was the largest entertainment P.R. firm in the world. I even ran my own agency a couple of times. Currently I'm vice president at Weissman/Markovitz Communications, formerly Murray Weissman & Associates, a boutique agency with major clients, including Paramount, Fox, Lionsgate, Miramax, the Weinstein Company and AMC. We served as public relations consultants for Lionsgate on the Oscar-winning "Crash." I've worked as a motion picture peon and as an executive.

During the course of all this I have made my home in London, Paris, Munich, Brussels and, for the past 35 years, California. This potpourri background has given me the insight of an insider and an outsider, a participant and an observer.

Leonard Morpurgo
Los Angeles, 2009

***

HONEYMOONS

One spring morning in 1965 I received a phone call in my Paris office from Columbia's headquarters in New York. They had a task for me, a very special task, a most delicate task. My job would be to avoid publicity at all costs.

"All right," I said. "So what is this mysterious assignment?"

I was told that Cary Grant was going to star in Columbia Pictures' "Walk, Don't Run" later that year. In the meantime, the studio wanted to take the best possible care of him. He had just married a young actress named Dyan Cannon and they were about to leave Los Angeles for England to visit his 90-year-old mother living in Bristol. They then planned to honeymoon in Paris for several days and I had been selected to look after them while they were in the City of Lights.

"Do whatever he asks and stay with him as long as he needs you."

I was also instructed to drive him wherever he wanted to go in my own car. He didn't want to hire a limo because that could be a breach of security. For the same reason, he would not be staying at a hotel, but in a friend's apartment. Secrecy was of the utmost importance.

Columbia's desire to please Grant was understandable. The 61-year-old actor was still Hollywood's biggest name and a star of almost mythic proportions. I had, at that time, never heard of his 28-year-old bride. Nobody realized that "Walk, Don't Run" would be his last movie. Grant was a romantic leading man and felt that he had become too old for that kind of role. He had no desire, nor financial need, to become a character actor.

[This would not be my first time meeting Cary Grant. Some four years earlier, in early 1961, when I'd been working in the industry only a few months, I had visited him at Pinewood Studios, outside London He was filming "The Grass Is Greener" with Deborah Kerr, Jean Simmons, and Robert Mitchum. At the time I was working in the press office at Rank Film Distributors and had brought some journalists to the set.

I recall sitting alone with Grant in his dressing room at that time when he remarked on the way I was holding my hands folded together.

"You know, that's a very good sign about your character. It shows that you are a properly balanced person—equal parts male and female," he said, smiling.

I was too flattered that Cary Grant would notice me at all to think about what he had said. Later it dawned on me that he was inferring I could be bi-sexual. If I had been, I would have picked up on it at the time, but I wasn't and I didn't. It does, however, seem to indicate Cary's own sexual interests.]

I met Cary and Dyan at Orly Airport in my battered old Renault Dauphine and drove them to an apartment on the rue du Bac, on the left bank. He was the charming, friendly Cary Grant of the screen, his silver hair brushed back, an ascot at his throat. Dyan's lovely face was framed by blonde hair. Her dress clung to her body. She smiled a greeting when I introduced myself, but didn't have much to say. Cary did the talking.

Their friend's second floor apartment was high-ceilinged and spacious, with a fireplace in the living room and rugs scattered on the hardwood floor.

Cary told me they would be staying for four days and he wanted me with them at all times. This seemed strange. After all, the man was on his honeymoon with a beautiful young bride. Why would they want a third person traipsing along? I think there had to be two reasons. As a star for so many years he wasn't used to handling such chores as booking restaurants or driving a car. I also had the feeling that he was uncomfortable alone with Dyan. He saw her as a child bride and had married her for only one reason—to provide him with his first progeny. At his age this could be his last opportunity. In fact, his daughter Jennifer, born exactly nine months after this honeymoon, WAS his only offspring. Today she is a respected actress herself.

I was told to find quiet, inexpensive places for lunch and dinner. He did not want to go to any "in" restaurants where he would be spotted. So I took them to places where I'd go myself on my then meager salary.

He became upset only once. We went to a quaint old restaurant on the Ile Saint Louis with a prix fixe of 30 francs ($6) a head. Even back then, this

OF KINGS AND QUEENS AND MOVIE STARS

was not considered an expensive restaurant. Nevertheless, he was furious.

"How could you have me eat at such an expensive place?" he demanded.

I was taken aback until I remembered the rumors I'd heard about his tightness with money. I began to think using my car instead of a limousine and the apartment instead of a hotel, were matters of frugality rather than secrecy.

The following day I took him to L'Etoile D'Or, a small restaurant on the Avenue Carnot, round the corner from my office. I was used to going there a couple of times a week. The cost of a lunch was about five francs ($1). Here Cary Grant was happy. He went nuts over the haricots vert, saying he had never tasted such fresh and delicious vegetables. As we were leaving, the proprietor, Monsieur Constantin, asked me if I could possibly obtain Mr. Grant's autograph for him. Cary said he would do better than that. When he returned to Hollywood he'd send an autographed photo.

Cary and Dyan were alone for just one meal during their stay in Paris. They took a cab into a working class neighborhood, had what they described as a wonderful meal, but refused to tell me the name of the restaurant.

"That would spoil the place. It would never be the same," he said.

At the time I thought he was exaggerating, but a few weeks later I understood the power of his name. True to his word, he sent an autographed 8x10 for the Constantins. Two weeks after I gave them the still, they closed the restaurant for renovation. When they reopened a month later the local bistro had become a chic restaurant and the prices were more than doubled. The Cary Grant photo was on the wall. I could never afford to eat there again. Soon, photos of other stars adorned the walls of L'Etoile D'Or, but Cary Grant's picture remained in solitary splendor with a wall to itself.

[I returned to the restaurant in 1992. Constantin had remarried but had later died of a heart attack. I met his widow who was now running the restaurant with her new husband. The Cary Grant photo was still there, but she knew little of its history. She was delighted to learn about its origin.]

The more time I spent with Cary Grant the stranger I found him to be. He seemed to be playing various roles all the time, as if afraid to be himself. He spent much of his time with Dyan playing the child's word guessing game, Hangman. They had no real conversations in my presence. When he and I talked it was often about deep philosophical subjects. He was like a chameleon, acting out parts that he thought were suitable for the person he was with. I felt sorry for Dyan. Here she was, married to the most famous movie star in the world and she was nothing more than a plaything.

One day I asked to be excused. The work was piling up at the office and my boss, Jack Wiener, not the calmest of men, wasn't happy that I was neglecting it. I hadn't been there more than an hour when my secretary rushed in, her face flushed with excitement. Cary was on the phone.

"Leonard," he said. "Dyan and I are at a café by the Seine. I want to take her for a ride on the Bateau Mouche to show her where I filmed "Charade" with Audrey Hepburn. We need you to smuggle us on board."

So, to Jack Wiener's considerable annoyance, I drove to the right bank café he had named and walked with them across the road to the glass-walled tourist boat, the Bateau Mouche, where some of the classic scenes in "Charade" were filmed. Cary wore a hat, sunglasses and a raincoat that covered his ears. I spoke to the boat's captain who kindly allowed us to board at the stern while tourists were being boarded forward. We sat there quietly by ourselves and went unrecognized.

The only time I noticed any sexual attraction between them was one evening after dinner when Dyan and I were sitting by the fire in their apartment living room. Cary walked by in his underpants.

"My God! A naked man!" Dyan joked. She told me it was time for me to go home. I was happy to leave.

On their last night in town, Cary said they had no need to hide any more. They'd be gone in the morning, so any publicity would be too late to affect them. He wanted to go to the Brasserie Lipp, an historic restaurant on the Boulevard St. Germain, uniquely favored by politicians, artists, writers and entertainers. Within 24 hours of being seen there, all of Paris would know.

I double parked my Renault on the corner of St. Germain des Prés and asked Cary to wait there while I checked out the place with Dyan. It was 8:30 p.m., when it would normally be impossible to get a table chez Lipp. We were met at the door by the maitre d'hotel.

"I am from Columbia Pictures. The lady with me is Mrs. Cary Grant.

Mr. Grant is waiting in my car outside. We would like a table," I said, reveling in the moment.

The maitre d's eyes widened momentarily. "But of course, Monsieur," he said.

Dyan waited while I returned to the car and told Cary that we had a table. We left the car double-parked and I led Cary the few yards to the restaurant. I followed the two of them as we were guided to a table in the rear of the restaurant and was amused by the gasps from other patrons as we worked our way through the room. Even in this place where prime ministers and prima donnas could dine without turning a head, Cary Grant was someone special.

Brasserie Lipp is a restaurant of strict hierarchy. Miraculously, the number one table, known as La Rotonde, was available and we were seated there. I don't know whom they had kicked out or where they were sitting, but it had all been done in two or three minutes.

When I later received a letter from Cary, which he obviously typed himself, I was initially peeved because he had not even remembered my name correctly. Then I saw he had also spelled his wife's name incorrectly—and felt a little better. Here is that letter.

Dear Leon,

Here is the photograph for your friends, the proprietors of L'Etoile d'Or. Since they didn't give you their first names I merely signed it to <u>The</u> Constantins.

Anyway, and more importantly, it brings with it Diane's and my affectionate and appreciative thoughts to you for all your kindness and trouble on our behalf and for your constantly cheerful company.

Our journey back—to a surprisingly humid California—was restful and undisturbed and things couldn't have gone better. Thank you, Leon, and please thank anyone else who so kindly helped our need for a few happily unpublicized days in Paris.

With fond and grateful thoughts to Jack [Wiener] and a few relaxed deep breaths for each morning and evenings—and between times too.

P.S. Why do we call you Leonard? It's Leon, isn't it? Isn't it?

I met Dyan again more than 40 years later at a studio party a couple of days before the 2008 Academy Awards. We talked about that long-ago experience and, though I could sense that there had been painful times, she defended Cary.

"He taught me a lot and he did give me my beautiful daughter, Jennifer," she said. Dyan told me that she was writing a book about those years. She was sure that I would find it very interesting.

***

Having been on Cary Grant's honeymoon with *his* wife, I balanced the books six years later by going on my own honeymoon without *my* wife.

Explanation forthcoming.

I met my second wife Jacqueline in Paris in January of 1971. A couple of nights earlier I had met a beautiful African-American model named Bobbie and offered her tickets to the premiere of "The Owl and the Pussycat". I couldn't go with her, I explained, because it was on a Friday and Fridays were my tennis nights. Nothing came between me and my tennis.

Hah! I reckoned without her determination.

She told me that she had a couple of girlfriends, a Jugoslav model and an American writer. She wanted tickets for them too and insisted that I join them.

I weakened. Three beautiful women. Maybe I could miss tennis for one week.

I showed up at Bobbie's apartment at the same time as a rotund gentleman with a wooden leg. We looked at each other and smiled awkwardly. The door was opened by an attractive American woman in her early thirties. She explained that Bobbie was "indisposed." I found out later that she had been in a fight with her ex-husband and was nursing her wounds. I never even saw her. Instead I ended up escorting the Jugoslav model and the American woman to the theater and we arranged to meet "wooden-leg" at a restaurant later. Apparently he had the hots for the model. I developed the hots for the American whose name was Jacqueline.

We fell in love and six months later were married in Meudon, the quiet town in which I lived, halfway between Paris and Versailles. We'd booked a hotel in Spain for our honeymoon.

OF KINGS AND QUEENS AND MOVIE STARS 9

A couple of weeks before the wedding, I got word from Columbia Pictures' head office in New York that Stanley Kramer, the director ("Judgement at Nuremburg") would be coming to Paris for a couple of days before going on to the Berlin Film Festival. A week after Berlin he would be at the Moscow Film Festival. They wanted me to meet him at the Paris airport and accompany him on his festival tour. There was only one problem. His flight was due the day and exact hour of my wedding.

Surely somebody else in the Paris office could handle this. No, I was told, "it has to be you." This sounded like a cue for a song, but I was in no mood for singing.

"What about my honeymoon? I've already paid the deposit."

"You'll have to cancel it. We will, of course, pay you the amount of the deposit if you can't get a refund."

Big deal!

Naturally, Jacqueline wasn't too pleased to learn that not only would there be no honeymoon, but I wouldn't even be with her for four out of the next five weeks. Great start to a marriage!

I figured that at the very least Stanley Kramer could find his own way from the airport to his hotel. I may have lost my honeymoon, but I wasn't about to screw up my own wedding just to greet some director.

I called him the evening of his arrival and apologized for not being there to meet him.

"I had something more important to do. I was getting married."

Stanley was chagrined to learn how he had messed up my plans. He apologized and invited my wife and me to join him and his wife for lunch two days later at Fouquets, a chic restaurant on the corner of the Champs Elysees and Avenue George V. It was a pleasant lunch, though marred by the knowledge that I would be leaving the country the following day. Jacqueline took it very well, all in all.

The film we were promoting at both festivals was "Bless the Beasts and Children" which was well received but won no awards.

While we were in Berlin, Stanley made a very generous offer. He was really upset that he'd unwittingly interfered with our plans and wanted to give us a wedding gift—a round trip ticket from Paris to Moscow for Jacqueline. Gratefully I accepted and phoned Jacqueline in Paris with the good news. I told her that she should quickly apply for a visa from the Soviet Embassy.

We left Berlin for a week in Paris before going on to Moscow. I had been home two days when disaster struck. Jacqueline became sick and had to be hospitalized. We didn't know if she would be out of the hospital and well enough to travel, but I still pursued that visa. Two days before I was due to leave, the doctors said she would be well enough to travel and the Soviets gave me a visa.

Disaster averted? Unfortunately not.

I made the mistake of telling Marion Jordan, who at that time was head of Columbia's foreign distribution out of New York, that my wife would be joining us in Moscow.

"No wives," he said curtly.

Angrily, I protested. He'd screwed up my honeymoon and now he was doing this.

"This is a business trip and no wives are allowed. Besides, if you accept this gift, you will be indebted to Kramer and he will think you're working for him. Our other producers will suffer. You must return the ticket."

This was nonsense and I told him so. I would give Kramer 100 per cent effort, but so would I the other filmmakers we were representing at the festival.

Jordan was adamant. I almost quit Columbia right there, but common sense prevailed.

I was furious and became even more annoyed when Jordan showed up in Moscow with his own wife.

Jacqueline, meantime, had left Paris the same day as I, to spend the two weeks with my parents in London. At least it gave her a chance to get to know Ralph and Maurice, my older brothers. It was a pleasant trip for her, but not exactly what we had had in mind.

***

This next story is not really about a honeymoon, but close enough.

In August of 1961 I traveled from London to Hull in Yorkshire, to marry my first wife, Valerie, a pretty Yorkshire brunette. I had met her at a party on the eve of my 28th birthday. We honeymooned in Italy. Two weeks later,

OF KINGS AND QUEENS AND MOVIE STARS

I was sent on my first assignment abroad by Rank Film Distributors, for whom I was working at the time.

It wasn't a bad assignment; in fact it was very exciting. I was to escort Weston Taylor, show business editor for the News of the World, to Rome to interview Sophia Loren. We were about to open the film "El Cid" in which Loren starred with Charlton Heston.

Weston and I arrived in Rome only to find that La Loren had been unexpectedly detained in New York. She sent her regrets, but would be in Rome four days later and would be happy to meet with us then.

Weston and I called our respective offices and asked permission to stay on in Rome until she arrived. Permission granted.

So there I was, in Rome for the first time in my life, sightseeing with a good friend at company expense. Not a bad way to compensate for being away from my bride.

We did all the tourist stuff, the Coliseum, the Via Veneto and, of course, the best restaurants on my expense account.

Weston was a circus buff. I'm not, but nevertheless agreed to accompany him to the circus that was installed in one of the city's suburbs.

On the bus on the way back to the hotel, a conversation took place which has puzzled me ever since. It was late in the evening and the bus was almost empty. The bus conductor struck up a conversation.

"Nice to be in Rome to see Sophia Loren, isn't it?" he said.

"How did you know we're here to see her?" I asked in astonishment.

"I read in paper," he replied.

Our trip was hardly important enough to warrant an article in a Rome newspaper and nobody had taken our photographs anyway. It was a puzzle then and still is today.

Finally, Sophia Loren arrived and we took a cab (no buses this time) to the palazzo she shared with her husband, Carlo Ponti.

We had tea together and Sophia was delightful. At this time she was 27 years old and at the height of her career. She was also gorgeous and wore a black number that showed off her generous figure. Her living room was filled with exquisite furniture, paintings and ornaments. She served us tea from a silver tea set. Every now and then the interview would be interrupted by a phone call to or from her husband, who was working in another part of the house. There was a lot of "caro mio" and kisses blown into the phone.

Weston told her that I had only recently married myself. He joked that Sophia Loren was the only woman in the world I would leave my wife for.

She asked me my wife's name. I told her.

"Poor Valeria," she said. "All alone in London."

She asked if I had a photo of her. Of course I did and showed it proudly.

"Oh, she is beautiful. I would very much like to meet her the next time I am in London."

Needless to say, when I returned home the next day I proudly told Valerie what Sophia had said.

Three years later that conversation came back to haunt me. Our marriage had floundered and by this time I was living alone in Paris. Valerie sued me for judicial separation. At the London hearing she put a different slant on the conversation. She claimed that I had boasted Loren wanted to have an affair with me. She also brought the name of Princess Margaret into the picture, an equally absurd allegation. Fortunately, the judge saw that this was nonsense and threw out her case after four days of hearings. When I left the Law Courts a phalanx of Fleet Street photographers was waiting. I was used to working with large groups of photographers, but this was the first time I'd been the object of their lenses.

***

A ROYAL PAIN

I was to spend more than 10 years in Paris, off and on, and it became one of the most exciting times of my life. Though I moved from there some 35 years ago it's still the one place I miss. To me this city IS Europe, everything else a cheap imitation. Yes, the Parisians are rude, but then they're rude to everyone. No need to take it personally. I enjoy the sophistication, not just the food, wine, clothing, but their entire attitude. The truth is, they just don't give a shit and that, at least, is honest.

One evening I was dining at L'Entrecôte where the French ate at that time. Now it is strictly for American tourists. My date and I started a conversation with a gentleman eating alone at the next table. Inevitably we got on to the hot topic of that time—President De Gaulle's veto of British admission to the European Economic Community. All my French friends thought it was a ridiculous and petty policy. This man, however, defended De Gaulle, throwing out facts and figures about agriculture, coal mines, industry to my total bewilderment.

I asked him how come he knew so much.

"It's my job," he explained.

"So what's your job?"

"I'm the President's advisor on European affairs."

"So you're the son of a bitch!" I heard myself saying.

"Yes, I'm the son of a bitch," he replied, grinning happily.

We'd both said what we felt and no offense had been taken. In fact, he ended up inviting my date and me back to his apartment and asked us to call up our friends and make a party of it.

***

One of the most memorable and nerve-wracking events in my life occurred one spring evening about three years after I had moved to Columbia Pictures' European head office in Paris.

A balmy breeze caressed its way across the Place Trocadero as if it were trying to calm my nerves. It didn't. I paced impatiently in front of the Palais de Chaillot. Where the hell was he!? Four hundred of France's elite, le tout Paris, as they were known, in the theater upstairs. Photographers from the world's media were waiting to pounce. The timing couldn't have been worse. It was mid May and all the other publicity executives were at the Cannes Film Festival. I was on my own.

At last the black Bentley rounded the corner and slid to a halt in front of me. I opened the door discreetly engraved with the initials "HRH" and the Duke and Duchess of Windsor stepped out. She wore a long, black evening gown. He wore the required black tie.

"Good evening, sir, ma'am" I said. "Lovely evening." They smiled to acknowledge my fatuous remark.

"Everything's ready. You have a full house," I continued. I bit down the impulse to tell him that I beat him with four of a kind and ushered them and the Duke's equerry ahead of me up the stairs. As we rounded the corner, a phalanx of flash bulbs popped. Frantically I waved at the photographers to hold off. The Duke had only just come out of the hospital following cataract surgery and his eyes were extremely sensitive to light. I was ignored.

"Turn those lights off," he yelled. He was ignored too.

He continued. "I said turn those bloody lights off. I don't need any publicity. Don't you know who I am! I was the King of England."

Oh, shit! The man was drunk. He'd been at the J&B again.

I ushered the royal couple to their seats at the front of the auditorium, followed by a dozen photographers. The Duke stood up and started yelling again. I pushed a group of photographers out of one door only to see them come through another. I tried to catch the eye of the projectionist in his booth, waving my arm so that he could start the film. Finally the house lights dimmed and the picture started. One more rebellious flashlight blazed before I could get the doors closed. Then I had to face a grumbling press corps. Why were they invited if they couldn't do their job? I promised them a ten minute session when the film was over, though I had no idea if I'd be able to keep that promise. Meanwhile they were welcome to enjoy the bar. That should keep them quiet.

The film that was causing all this uproar was a documentary about

OF KINGS AND QUEENS AND MOVIE STARS 15

the Duke and Duchess entitled "A King's Story", produced by American expatriate, Jack Le Vien, for Columbia Pictures. The Duke had reigned as Edward VIII, King of Great Britain and Emperor of India, for less than a year, abdicating on December 11, 1936, even before his coronation could take place. Britain had become scandalized by his romance with a married American woman, Wallis Simpson. She divorced, but the country could not accept his marrying a divorced woman. His father, George V, had renamed the Royal Family the House of Windsor and he thus took that name after the abdication. The film told this story, closing with his moving abdication speech.

Numerous documentaries had been made about the Windsors, but this was the first one in which he'd been actively involved himself. He had provided an eloquent prologue and epilogue, filmed in the garden of their beautiful home in the Bois de Boulogne in Paris.

The screening took place in 1965. I had planned the event over several weeks "aided" by the Duchess of Windsor who was very much in charge of this particular household. The screening had originally been set for the Publicis private theater on the Champs Elysees, but the Duchess's guest list of 80 just grewed and grewed, so we changed the venue to the larger Palais de Chaillot.

The Duchess became involved in the minutest details of the operation. We went over the guest list again and again. She planned every hors d'oeuvre and most important, insisted that there be plenty of J&B whisky, which was all that the Duke drank.

The already difficult evening was made even more nerve-wracking by the presence of Abe Schneider, President of Columbia Pictures, in town from New York. Though I had worked for the studio for four years, this was the first time I'd met Schneider.

I was confused. Who took precedence, my President or my King? (I was born in England).

When the house lights came on at the end of the screening I rushed to my erstwhile king, still seated on his "throne." I was fearful that there'd be another scene, but he had sobered up. He was dabbing his eyes.

What did he think of the film?

"Wonderful!" he said. "I don't mind admitting, Leonard, that it made me cry."

A photographer had followed me to the royal seat and captured that moment on film. The photo later appeared in all the world's major publications. When I asked, somewhat belatedly, if the photographers could stay for ten minutes, the Duke said, magnanimously, "Of course, let 'em take all the time they want."

I made sure he had a glass of scotch in his hand and set up a photo with him talking to Abe Schneider and with Arlene Dahl, the token representative of Hollywood stardom.

Finally, with much hand shaking and royal waving, the Duke and Duchess left and, as the tension of the moment faded, my legs started shaking like two sticks of jelly.

***

In the following months I became friendly with the Windsors. They invited me to their home and I invited them to private screenings of films I thought would interest them.

One day I received a call from Jack Le Vien in London. Apparently he had just spoken to the Duke who told him that he had seen the film "Ship of Fools." The movie had not yet been released and Le Vien pointed this out.

"How did you get to see it?" he asked.

"I was invited by my friend," said the Duke.

"Which friend would that be?"

"Leonard Morpurgo."

"Hrmph!" I retorted when Le Vien told me this. "What a name dropper!"

***

Some time later, the Duke's equerry asked me if I could set up a screening. They had received from the States a 16mm black and white print of yet another documentary on his life and he was curious to see it. I blocked off a couple of hours the next afternoon at a small private screening room on the Champs Elysees. The Duke and his equerry arrived on time and the three of us sat down to watch the familiar story unfold on the screen.

OF KINGS AND QUEENS AND MOVIE STARS 17

Probably the man most responsible for forcing the abdication of Edward VIII was the British Prime Minister, Stanley Baldwin. When Baldwin appeared on the screen the Duke turned to me and blew a very loud, and most royal, raspberry.

***

Being in the presence of any European royalty can make the most hardened sophisticate feel nervous. By far the most intimidating sovereign is the Queen of England. I have attended numerous royal premieres in London, usually held at the Odeon Theatre, Leicester Square, at that time flagship of the Rank Theatre chain. When the Queen enters the magnificent upstairs lobby to be introduced to the waiting line of celebrities, the silence is so stifling that you wonder so many important people could be so quiet. There is no shuffling of feet, no murmured voices or scratchy cough. Nobody seems to be even breathing. Then come the quiet questions and nervous answers as the Queen makes her way down the line. The men in black or white tie, bow their heads, the women in elegant décolleté, curtsy. As the Queen moves on to the royal box, sound erupts like water cascading through a broken levee.

***

My personal calvary of embarrassment came in the presence of King Baudouin and Queen Fabiola of Belgium in 1967. I was at this time living in Munich, supervising publicity for Columbia Pictures in the southern part of Europe. I was asked to move to Brussels for four months to find and train a new publicity manager there and to organize a couple of major premieres.

One of these events was the royal premiere of "A Man For All Seasons." At first there were some doubts whether the film would even be suitable for royal viewing. After all, it did concern England's Henry VIII who went around chopping off his wives' heads and, what is more important in this Roman Catholic country, who had broken away from The Church. Eventually, the royal advisors decided that enough centuries had passed since the events depicted and it wouldn't be offensive to the Belgian king and queen.

Though Belgium is less than 12,000 square miles in size you can find a chasm there wider than the Atlantic Ocean. That abyss is the ethnic difference between the Flemish speaking Flemings in the North and the French speaking Walloons in the South. The Flems, whose language is a dialect of Dutch, are in the majority, yet they seem to have an inferiority complex that can drive them into a rage regarding anything French. This I found out to my chagrin at one of the regular meetings I attended with the directors of the Belgian Red Cross, the premiere's designated charity.

Most of the committee members were Flemings, yet because I was a foreigner and they knew I spoke French, they deigned to speak the detested language in my presence. At this particular meeting, which happened to be the last before the big night, they were talking among themselves in Flemish. Unthinkingly, I joined in the conversation. Through all these gatherings I'd neglected to tell them that I spoke fluent Dutch. Well, were they pissed!

"How could you make us speak that hated language all this time, when you speak Dutch?!" one of them screamed at me.

"I didn't think it was important," I replied.

"Not important?!" was his indignantly sputtered response.

I could have been telling him that his wife had been having an affair, such was his anger; though he may well have heard such a revelation with more equanimity.

The premiere itself was a success. After months of writing press releases, committee reports and designing printed programs in two languages, we had a full house. John Hurt, one of the stars, was among those who attended the black-tie evening. Five hundred guests, including the King and Queen, were invited to attend a cocktail reception at the theater following the screening.

I was among those who stood in line to be presented to the royal couple. Bobby Meyers, Columbia's manager in Belgium at that time, introduced me. The King shook my hand and moved on. The Queen made the mistake of asking me a question.

"You have an interesting last name," she said in English. "What is its origin?"

"It's Italian, ma'am," I said, still holding her hand.

"Oh, so your parents are from Italy."

"No, ma'am. They're Dutch," I said, sweat beading on my forehead. I still held her hand.

"Then you're Dutch."

"No, ma'am. I'm English," I said, a vein now throbbing at my temple. I still held her hand.

"And you live in Belgium?"

"No, ma'am. I live in Germany," I said miserably.

She disengaged herself from my nervous grip, shook her head in bewilderment and with a twitch of a smile said, "My, you are international!"

***

Fast-forward 30 years. Bobby Meyers, who has remained a friend of mine all this time, was at the 1997 Cannes Film Festival. He was sitting in the bar of the Majestic Hotel when he noticed John Hurt sitting alone. He went up to him and introduced himself.

"I'm sure you won't remember the occasion, but I was the host at the Belgian premiere of 'A Man for All Seasons,' which you attended," said Bobby.

"As a matter of fact, I do remember that evening very well," said Hurt. "The moment that's stuck in my memory all these years was the image of this big time Hollywood executive sweating profusely when he met the Queen. Why on earth would someone like that be so nervous?"

Bobby laughed and explained the embarrassing situation in which this executive—me—had found himself. This is Bobby's favorite story and he's told it hundreds of times.

***

As I've just pointed out, anyone can get nervous in the presence of royalty.

Following an unbelievable night out on the town in which we savored all the delights that Stockholm could offer, I escorted producer/director, Carl Foreman and two of the stars, George Hamilton, who, as always, was remarkably handsome, and Senta Berger a beautiful 22-year-old Austrian actress, to the Swedish premiere of "The Victors." They were to be presented to King Gustav, at the theater in Stockholm.

As we waited in the bar of the Grand Hotel that evening, all of us still bleary-eyed, Carl confided to George that he was nervous about meeting the king.

"I have just the thing for you," said George, who carried a miniature pharmacy with him wherever he traveled. He went up to his room and a few minutes later returned with a couple of pills.

"Take these and in half an hour you'll feel great, Carl."

Foreman did as he was instructed and, indeed, half an hour later admitted that he was totally relaxed.

"I feel wonderful," he said. "Nothing could bother me now. There's just one problem. My face muscles are so relaxed I can't keep my dentures in. Ah well."

Perhaps George Hamilton should have taken a couple of those pills himself. At the line-up he got a case of the royal nerves. When he was presented to King Gustav he exclaimed, "It's a majesty, your pleasure!"

***

Just one more royal story.

The occasion was the Dutch royal premiere of "Lawrence of Arabia." In fact, it was not only the premiere of the film, but also the opening night of the theater—the Euro Cinema, located in a suburb of The Hague.

I arrived in Holland a couple of weeks ahead of time and found, to my horror, that the theater was just a concrete shell. There was no way it was going to be ready. I bullied the theater owners and the contractors and they assured me that everything would be all right on the night. I'd heard that before.

To save the expense of manufacturing new neon lettering for the theater's facade, someone had the bright idea of shipping the "Lawrence of Arabia" neon sign from Paris, where the film had just finished its run. I opened the crates on an empty lot across from the theater. Carefully I unwrapped the letters, one by one. I pulled out an "L." It was broken. I pulled out an "a." It was broken. Every one of those damn neon letters was broken.

OF KINGS AND QUEENS AND MOVIE STARS

So, of course, I had to order a totally new sign from a manufacturer in Amsterdam. A rush order. Overtime.

Two days before the opening the theater was still without seats. The day of the premiere, carpet was still being hammered in. Half an hour before the opening workmen were still painting trim, while floral arrangements were set up.

Because Columbia's main office in the Netherlands was in Amsterdam, the drivers who would be ferrying our celebrities to and from their hotel were also from Amsterdam. So that I could be sure they would know the route, I had them make a practice run from the hotel to the theater. I didn't ask them to drive from the theater to the hotel. Remember that. It's important.

The night arrived and, as I'd been promised, a miracle had occurred and the theater was ready. Boy scouts lined the route on both sides of the road, holding flaming torches. Senior Columbia executives, the producer, Sam Spiegel and Omar Sharif, starring in his first English-speaking role, all made it to the theater safely.

Queen Juliana and her consort, Prince Bernhardt, arrived quietly and we took our seats, our brand new seats, in the auditorium.

The Dutch royal family is much more relaxed than the British. After all, they ride around town on their bicycles. It's hard to imagine Queen Elizabeth II doing that. (Come to think of it, with assassinations happening on the streets of Amsterdam these days, the Dutch royals probably aren't as free to go cycling anymore either.) So it was, that at the intermission, we all stood around chatting. When the bell rang signaling the beginning of the second half, Prince Bernhardt, who was smoking a cigarette, turned to one of the ushers and said, "Bring that ashtray to my seat, please."

As the usher started to obey, the Queen, giving her husband and the usher an intimidating look that even Dutch sovereigns can manage, said, "No! Other people are not permitted to smoke in the theater. You cannot be an exception. You have to obey the rules like everybody else."

"Yes, dear," said the chastened prince.

The film finished to a richly deserved applause. Outside, I ushered all of my celebrities into the fleet of cars, climbing into the last one myself with Columbia's Dutch manager, Rob Herzet. We arrived at the hotel, where a sumptuous reception was being held.

As the minutes went by, I began to feel a sickly premonition. Sam Spiegel not the easiest of men, had not shown up and he had been in one of the first cars. Herzet was also worried. "I don't care about Spiegel," he said. "My wife's in that car."

Forty-five minutes later they arrived, Spiegel's face black with anger. He stormed up to his room, announcing that he had no intention of attending the party.

"Don't worry," said Omar Sharif, who had witnessed the scene. He'll calm down in a little while and I'll go get him myself." Which he did.

From Rob's wife, Tina, I learned what had happened. As soon as they were in the car, Spiegel had asked the driver if he knew where he was going. The driver had assured him that he did.

"Are you sure?"

"Yes, sir."

A few minutes later Spiegel again asked the driver if he knew the way. Spiegel was a man who could terrify far more assured people than that poor driver. So, in a self-fulfilling prophecy, Spiegel made the man so nervous that he really did get lost. Exploding with anger, Spiegel had the car stop in the middle of a busy thoroughfare and climbed out, followed by an unwilling Mrs. Herzet. There Spiegel stood, right in the road, refusing to budge until he had hailed a cab to take him to the hotel. He had not spoken another word until they arrived.

Witnesses to all this embarrassment were my parents, who had arrived from England to visit with Dutch members of the family. This was the only time I was ever able to invite them to a film event I had organized. My mother didn't care about Spiegel's rage or about unfinished theaters. She was not perturbed by all the last minute hassles. She got to shake Omar Sharif's hand. Now that was something to tell her friends when she returned home to England.

As "Lawrence of Arabia" has meant more to me than any other film I've worked on I've devoted an entire chapter to it later in this book.

***

EARLY DAYS

I almost failed to make this long journey through the byways and freeways of movie publicity. In fact, I very nearly didn't get out of first gear.

In late 1960, after a decade working as a journalist in England, I joined Rank Film Distributors as a writer in the press office, recommended there by a film producer I had interviewed a few times. After I'd been on the job a couple of months, my boss, an old Scot and ex-Fleet Street reporter, was fired. He had been missing for four days and someone was dispatched to his home to see if he was all right. He was found lying on his living room floor in a drunken stupor.

That very afternoon I went to the head of the publicity department, Johnny Fairbairn, and asked to be given the suddenly vacant position. He told me I didn't have enough experience.

"So let me run the department until you find someone who does have the experience."

He agreed and I was given the bureaucratic sounding title of press officer.

One of my very first tasks was to organize a trade press conference for Samuel Bronston, producer of "El Cid", who was flying in from his home in Spain. I'd never run a press conference before, but I had seen them on television and knew what they were supposed to look like. I had a head table with two chairs and a microphone, and arranged three rows of chairs for the journalists. A bar was set up in the back of the room. I stood back proudly to admire my handiwork.

Bronston arrived and I sat him down behind the mike. I opened the proceedings and asked for questions. Silence! Maybe they were shy. I pointed to a writer I knew and asked him if he wanted to ask anything. He shook his head. The seconds ticked by like hours. All the prodding in the world failed to elicit one question. Feeling abject misery, I closed my first press conference. Grim-faced, Bronston stormed out. Then the press did what they had come for in the first place—they elbowed their way to the bar.

When I asked why nobody had asked any questions, they explained that they knew everything there was to know about Samuel Bronston and "El Cid". One older reporter kindly told me that I should have dispensed with the mike, the table and the chairs and gone straight to the cocktails. I could have introduced the journalists to Bronston one at a time, while everyone had drinks in their hands, and they would all feel they were getting exclusive interviews. Bronston would have been a lot happier too.

Later I learned that he had gone to John Fairbairn and demanded that I be fired for incompetence. Johnny refused, saying that it was his own fault for allowing me to run the event by myself without his being there. If I were fired, he would resign, he told the angry producer. I've always remembered Johnny's gesture with deep appreciation.

Rank never did find anybody ready to take over the press department at the salary they were offering and eventually, after about a year, I quit when Fairbairn's successor refused to give me a raise.

***

Charlton Heston arrived in town not long afterwards for the premiere of "El Cid." I was impressed by him and not only because I was talking to Moses in person.

When we met at Heathrow Airport he greeted me by name before I could tell him who I was. He had been briefed in Los Angeles. At the hotel I told him his first interview was in a couple of hours.

"That's fine," he said. "I'm going to take a nap. Please wake me when the journalist arrives."

I did as he asked and, though he had been sleeping soundly, he was fully awake in an instant and ready for the interview. He did this throughout the day, grabbing 10 or 20 minutes of sleep between each interview, always wide awake immediately. This is an unusual gift, being able to catnap anywhere, any time.

I wish I had such kind thoughts about Heston today. As the rabid former head of the National Rifle Association he represented the one facet of American life that I abhor.

***

OF KINGS AND QUEENS AND MOVIE STARS

The first Hollywood star I ever had dealings with was Kirk Douglas, visiting London for the premiere of "Spartacus". He stayed at the posh Claridges Hotel.

I remember being terribly impressed by him too when all he ordered for lunch was a dozen oysters and a bottle of champagne. I'd never seen anyone eat oysters before and they hardly seemed enough for an entire meal. Until that moment, my idea of a fancy lunch was roast beef and Yorkshire pudding and as much of it as I could get.

***

BULLIES

Most people are easy to get along with, but some take a little special handling. One of the most infamous Hollywood bullies was Otto Preminger, Hollywood's first genuine independent producer/director and sometime actor. With his thick Viennese accent and billiard ball head, he sounded and looked the part; a sort of latter-day Erich von Stroheim. It was an image that he relished. Many of the Preminger stories are apocryphal, but it's certain that he made various actors, male and female, cry and he was known to call them cattle.

I had the "pleasure" of working with Preminger on three occasions. One of the first major stunts I arranged after joining Columbia Pictures' London office was for the 1962 premiere of his "Advise and Consent". The film was a political drama set in Washington D.C. with an impressive cast including Henry Fonda, Charles Laughton, Don Murray, Walter Pigeon, Peter Lawford, Gene Tierney, Franchot Tone and Lew Ayres.

We had organized a post premiere party for about a thousand people at the elegant Café Royal on Regent Street. As the guests arrived they were given copies of that day's London Evening News. It was genuine except that the front page headline screamed:

PRESIDENT 'BACKS A RED'

U.S. Secretary Of State Nominee Alleged To Be A Communist

With the help of the newspaper's editorial staff I had written a phony front page. I was able to use photos of most of the cast with stories about their characters as if they really were president and senators. The challenge was to get in a photo of producer/director Preminger. This is the caption to that photo.

Film producer Otto Preminger was among the spectators at today's senate committee hearing. He is in Washington looking for material for a new film and he commented: "One day I may even make a film about this investigation."

The rest of the paper carried the usual sports, gossip and advertisements.

OF KINGS AND QUEENS AND MOVIE STARS 27

That evening, going home on the "tube", the London subway, I pretended to read it, allowing other travelers to see the front page. Surreptitiously I watched their surprised faces. I can only imagine what they told their families and friends when they arrived at their destinations.

After I'd worked with Preminger for the "Advise and Consent" opening, I met him again on the immense stage of the Paris Opera House, where we were preparing for the premiere of his film "The Cardinal". The stage at the Opera is so huge that you could fit the entire building of the Comedie Francaise on it; not that I know anybody who would want to do that. Being in that cavernous edifice can indeed be overwhelming.

Throw in a rampaging Preminger and it becomes downright intimidating.

This was an important event for Preminger. He had worked long and hard on this film and the Paris gala premiere could set the tone for the film's release throughout Europe. So he was wired—and I was in the way. He told me to find a phone book. I ran around the gigantic backstage area looking for a phone, a phone book, someone who worked there. Nothing. Nobody.

Within 30 seconds, or so it seemed, Preminger was screaming for me. "Where the hell is Morpurgo? I want that telephone book now, not next week."

Of course, the more he bellowed the more nervous I became and the harder it became to concentrate on the simple task of finding a phone book. Eventually, I located a backstage office with phone, phone book and even someone to hand it to me.

I returned to the stage to be screamed at some more.

I next encountered the redoubtable Otto Preminger in London. I had flown in from Paris with a dozen French journalists on a junket to visit the location shooting of his film, "Bunny Lake Is Missing". The thriller starred Laurence Olivier, Carol Lynley and Keir Dullea, all of whom had agreed to be interviewed.

While we were in London the unit was shooting nights. The location was Carlton House Terrace, a prestigious street in the center of London. However, the house which served as the film's base camp was due to be demolished once the film crew moved on. There was electricity, but no plumbing.

At about two in the morning I needed to use the facility. I asked one of the crew members where the toilet was.

"There ain't nothing 'ere, mate," he said. "You gotta go out of the 'ouse, turn left and then after about 50 feet you'll come to an alley. Go down that alley until you get to a courtyard. The loo's in there."

I thanked him for his directions, walked down the street and into the alley. It was completely dark. Suddenly, out of the gloom, came the stentorious voice of Otto Preminger.

"Und vere are you going, Mr. Colombia?" he intoned.

"Oh, hello, Mr. Preminger. I'm actually looking for the toilet," I said, surprised to find him lurking in the shadows.

"Come, follow me. I vill show you vere is the toilet," he said.

He led me down the alley to a wooden door at the back of a courtyard.

"There is your toilet."

I thanked him, then said, before I could stop myself, "You know, Mr. Preminger. You must be the world's most highly paid lavatory attendant."

Fortunately, he was in one of his better moods and roared with laughter.

***

I joined Columbia Pictures four years after the demise of the infamous Harry Cohn, so I never witnessed any of his outrageous behavior. But he was certainly not the only executive with a fearsome reputation.

I had been working in the London office less than a month, as assistant to advertising and publicity director, Pat Williamson, when it was whispered that Mo Rothman was coming to town. He was senior vice president in charge of international distribution, based in New York. Colleagues warned me that this man had been known to fire someone because he didn't like the color of his tie. Never, ever cross this man, I was told. In those days in England it was unheard of to lose your job for anything but the most venal behavior. Only in America were you held hostage to the caprices of your superiors. Now all this could start happening here.

I had a brief and uneventful meeting with him and, so far as I know, no one was fired as a result of his visit. Nevertheless, this tall, dark-haired Canadian carried an aura of ruthlessness that left us all nervous.

A year later I was being considered for the position of assistant to Jack Wiener, the head of European publicity and advertising, based in Paris. He had apparently been impressed by the way I handled myself at the press screening prior to the world premiere of "Lawrence of Arabia." I do recall that I spent a lot of time running up and down the aisles of the theater, trying to look busy and important. I guess it worked.

Jack had also heard that my marriage to Valerie had disintegrated and figured that I might like a change of scenery. I had been having the same thoughts myself and had resolved to ask if there was a position available at our Hollywood studios once all the excitement of the "Lawrence" world premiere was behind us. I hadn't considered Paris. I'd never even been there, but if I was going to start a new life it seemed like a good a place as any.

As I got home from work the day following the premiere I received a call from my boss, Pat Williamson. I was to put on my tux and come to a club in Regent Street where Columbia's various European managers were having a party. Jack Wiener wanted to meet me.

My stomach was doing back flips as I drove to the West End. I had a long wait. It wasn't until two a.m. that Jack took me to one side and started the interview. I suppose he liked what he saw because he asked me to come to Paris to see how I would fit in.

As luck would have it, Mo Rothman was in town and he decided to interview me himself. He sat behind Jack's large teak desk waiting for me like a brooding vulture. Without a word, he pointed to a chair in front of the desk. As I sat down, he leaned forward and sneered, "You're Pat Williamson's assistant in London and now you want to be Jack Wiener's assistant in Paris. What's the big difference?"

In a flash of instinct I realized that Rothman's menace was just an act. If he felt that he could intimidate you, you'd be mincemeat. If you stood up to him you'd earn his respect. I decided to stand up, at least metaphorically.

Leaning forward, I sneered back, "Nineteen countries, that's the difference."

He seemed momentarily taken aback. He knew, of course, that the European office was responsible for all countries in Western Europe and the Middle East. Britain was not considered part of Europe and the British liked it that way.

Rothman tried a different tack. He started asking some very personal questions that could have been embarrassing if I had let them. But I was on to him now. I yelled right back at him, turning the embarrassment into a weapon.

His verbal onslaught stopped as suddenly as it had begun. He leaned back in his chair and, with a slight smile, said, "If you can work as good as you can talk you have the job."

Mo and I have been on good terms ever since.

The last time I saw him was at the Cannes Film Festival some years ago. I had been hired by CBS three weeks previously. Mo gave me a message for the president of my division.

"Tell him he fucks too much," he instructed me.

"But I haven't even met the man yet," I protested.

"Doesn't matter. You tell him what I said," insisted Mo.

I didn't pass on the message right away, but I did eventually.

***

William Friedkin is not the easiest of men, or maybe I caught him at a bad time. He had just completed directing "Cruising", starring Al Pacino and Paul Sorvino. It was a controversial film which Lorimar, the production company, had been pushing to get into the 1980 Deauville Film Festival. With its difficult theme, depicting the harsh underbelly of a tough gay subculture, there had been some resistance from the festival organizers, but they had finally come round.

Deauville, a quiet resort on the Normandy coast of France, had been organizing this festival of American films for a number of years and it had grown into a prestigious event. It could also be a good launching pad for a film in France and neighboring countries.

So it was with joyful stride that I walked into Friedkin's office at MGM Studios in Culver City (today the same lot is Sony Pictures Studios) to bring him the glad tidings that the film had finally been accepted and, what was more, they were inviting him to attend. This latter had taken a certain amount of arm-twisting.

My bright mood was quickly deflated when he announced that there was no way he would allow his picture in the festival unless it was in the prestigious opening night spot. I told him I didn't think that would be possible.

"Then you have no film," he said.

So back I went to the festival people. I begged, I pleaded, I offered them my first-born. They'd let me know.

A week later the answer came back. They had angered a lot of other people, but yes, because the film had already been announced, they had changed things around and it would be shown on opening night.

With a sigh of relief, I gave Friedkin the news. I also told him we had had requests from a couple of other European countries that wanted him to visit while he was in Europe. Several days later he agreed, but told me he wanted a complete list of all media interviews two weeks before he left. I explained that these schedules were always last minute affairs, depending on the availability of the media.

"Then I won't go. The deal is off."

So, now into offering my second born, I was able to twist the metaphorical arms of the various publicity managers and provided him with the schedule he requested.

"I want the circulations of all print publications, viewing audiences of all electronic media. I want to know their political leanings, how they address major world topics and I want the name and background of every journalist I will meet."

Nobody had ever requested this level of information before and reporters were often assigned at the last minute. I told him this.

"Then I won't go. The deal is off," he said with his now familiar refrain.

Well, we did it. Got him everything he wanted. Proud of myself, I was. Drained, but proud.

"I will not feel comfortable unless I can have my own French publicist looking after me in Deauville. If you can't hire Yanou Collard I won't go."

So I called Yanou in Paris and she agreed to represent Friedkin.

It had been decided that I would leave for France two days before Friedkin to make absolutely, positively sure that everything was on track. On the morning of my departure I dropped into Friedkin's office to say good-bye.

He was in a furious mood.

"This whole thing is fucked up!" he said.

I looked at him in amazement. After all the weeks of giving in to his every demand and on the very day I was leaving he had come up with this. I tried to stay calm.

"What exactly is the problem?"

"It's just fucked up. Things are not being organized properly, Yanou doesn't know what she's doing and I know it will be a disaster?"

I pointed out that Yanou was one of France's most prestigious publicists and she had been retained at his request. If he could give me just one example of where things were going wrong.

"I don't need to give examples. I'm not going and that is final!"

It occurred to me at that moment that Friedkin had never had any intention of going. He had kept putting up roadblocks, trying to scuttle the junket and finally, when that didn't work, he was just refusing to go. No reason.

I stormed out of the office, shaking with anger. That afternoon I had to undo all the preparations we had been working on for weeks. I canceled my own trip, telexed Deauville, Yanou Collard and the other European publicists who had all worked so hard to comply with his impossible demands.

The next day, Friedkin's secretary called me. She had seen my face when I left his office and it had worried her so much that she hadn't slept that night. I assured her that I was fine. I never saw Friedkin again.

***

ROMANCE

From an unpleasant memory we move to a most enjoyable episode that took place some 13 years earlier.

It all began in San Sebastian, a beautiful city in northwest Spain, situated on the Bay of Biscay. Each summer it is the site of the San Sebastian International Film Festival. I've been there only once, in June 1963. At that time its lovely beach, known as La Concha, or The Shell, was unspoiled. Its citizens had not yet become cynical and its annual homage to the film industry was still the highlight of their year. I'd like to think that it's still that way.

This was my first ever film festival and, 45 years later, I still recall the occasion with fondness.

Columbia Pictures had two films in competition and I was taking care of their stars—Nicole Courcel, who was in the French film, "Un Dimanche de Ville D'Avray" and Leslie Caron, star of the British picture, "The L Shaped Room."

On my arrival at the elegant hotel that served as the festival's headquarters, I was taken aside by the event's master of ceremonies, Spain's most famous bullfighter, whose main claim to fame outside his own country was his tempestuous affair with Ava Gardner.

It seems his predilections hadn't changed over the years.

"I want you to promise me something," he said. "You can have Nicole Courcel, but please leave Leslie Caron for me. I desire her greatly."

"Sure, be my guest," I replied magnanimously. Hell, I was as likely to end up with either one of them as fly to the moon.

His game seemed childish to me, though I was flattered that he thought I could be a player. I suppose I'd come a long way since my teenage years when I would blush if I had to speak to a girl. As it happens, I would blush at about anything when I was a teenager. I was a shy kid. I didn't even want to answer the telephone at home in case there'd be a stranger on the line. So my first job was as a "telephone reporter" in the sports room of

London's biggest circulation evening paper. Then I became a reporter on a local paper. That got rid of the shys in a hurry.

Back in San Sebastian the bullfighter did flirt outrageously with Leslie, but she kept a polite distance.

I had to stick closely to the two actresses when they ventured on to the streets. Wherever we went we were besieged by hordes of young autograph hunters. They even wanted my autograph. When I told them I wasn't anybody famous they just held out their pens and autograph books and shouted "Please! Please!" even louder. Sometimes I would sign my own name. At other times I'd sign the name of some Hollywood movie star. They never knew the difference.

Five months later "The L Shaped Room" was due to open in Copenhagen. I decided to call Leslie Caron at home to see if she would attend the opening. At that time she was married to Peter Hall, director of the Royal Shakespeare Company and lived with him in England. To my surprise she said she would be delighted to go to Denmark.

I was there to meet Leslie at Copenhagen Airport and together we drove to the Royal SAS Hotel. The premiere was the following evening and the day was to be filled with media interviews. This first evening was free of any official engagements.

We went to a restaurant with a dance floor and a live band. After the first course I asked her to dance. As we stepped on to the floor, the group stopped playing and started in on the title song of one of Leslie's movies—"Lili". It was in a Viennese waltz tempo. The other dancers had stopped to watch us.

"I can't dance the friggin' quick waltz," I whispered frantically in her ear. I felt my face redden in embarrassment as I stumbled and tripped over her feet. I still remembered how to blush. Here I was with one of the most beautiful and famous dancers in the world and I was making an ass of myself.

She grinned and suggested that we sit. I nodded thankfully.

We returned to the hotel and I escorted her to her suite. At her door I kissed her on the cheek.

"Was that a goodbye kiss or a hello kiss?" she asked.

I couldn't believe what I was hearing. It was fantasy time.

OF KINGS AND QUEENS AND MOVIE STARS

"Er, um, I guess it was a hello kiss," I stammered.

"Good," she said with a smile, opening the door.

I followed her inside, nonchalantly throwing my hat at the hat rack across the room. I missed. I didn't care.

The following morning Columbia's local publicity manager called Leslie to ask if she had heard from me. I couldn't be found anywhere.

"Not a word." Hanging up, she said, "That was for you."

Leslie was great with the press that day, keeping up a busy schedule. The Danish audience loved the movie and that evening I hosted a party in her honor. About 30 local theater owners and other film community dignitaries attended.

The date was November 22nd, 1963.

I was dancing with Leslie (not a Viennese waltz) when Columbia's manager in Denmark, Axel Jespersen, came up to me and whispered in my ear.

"Don't tell Miss Caron, but we just heard on the radio that President Kennedy has been shot." It seems he felt that she should be protected from bad news.

Of course I told her. We returned to the table to join our guests where we all sat silently. After a while a waiter told us Kennedy was dead.

This was no time to be partying. I suggested everyone should return to their homes. Leslie and I went back to the hotel.

A few months later she and I were sitting in the bar of the Plaza Athenee Hotel in Paris. She explained that she had something important to tell me. Apparently our tryst in Copenhagen had resulted in an unexpected and unwanted pregnancy. She told me that I was not to worry, however. She had gone to Switzerland and had a discreet abortion.

My mind whirled at the news. Part of me was excited to know that I was capable of fathering a child and another was sad that the fetus had been aborted before I even knew of its existence. Yet in another corner of my mind I felt relief that she had been in a position to take care of the matter.

While I was digesting this startling news a waiter came over to our table to tell Leslie that there was a long distance phone call for her.

When she returned she told me, "That was Universal Studios in Hollywood. They want me to star in a picture called "Father Goose" with

Cary Grant. I have to leave next week."

While in California, Leslie met Warren Beatty and they became an item. Well I knew it couldn't last.

I should point out that I wasn't married at this time. Nor was I married while having any of the other amorous adventures described elsewhere in this book.

***

In 1965 I was assigned to handle the publicity at the Venice Film Festival for a film directed by Arthur Penn. It was "Mickey One". Both Penn and the film's star, Warren Beatty, would be in attendance.

Beatty was staying in Paris at the George V Hotel before going on to Italy. I called him to introduce myself. Leslie Caron answered the phone.

"Guess who's going to be taking care of Warren in Venice," I told her.

"Oh, no. Not you!"

A few days later I was nervously waiting at Venice Airport to take Warren to the Excelsior Lido Hotel.

When we met, he said, "So you're Leonard. Welcome to the club!"

I was disgusted by his crudeness. Or maybe I was just a prude.

One afternoon I was sitting with Warren in the lobby of the Excelsior when a Finnish journalist whose name was Rita, asked for an interview. He would be delighted to give her one, he told her, pointing to the door of his room, which was adjacent to the lobby.

"Please go in there and I'll join you in a few minutes," he said.

"No thank you. I don't do interviews in bedrooms," she retorted.

Now this was a challenge for Warren. Women just did not turn him down. But he had met his match in Rita. In her typical independent Nordic fashion she withstood all his advances. She and I, however, became very close.

Beatty pursued her for weeks. Finally, at the London Hilton, the inevitable happened.

"Was it worth it?" I asked her later.

"Oh, yes!"

***

MORE "LAWRENCE"

Of all the hundreds of films with which I have been associated, "Lawrence of Arabia" is the one of which I am most proud. Of course, I don't have any right to be proud as I had absolutely nothing to do with its creation. Nevertheless, after more than a year of marketing, promoting and publicizing the film throughout Europe I did feel some involvement.

More than 40 years after its world premiere at the Odeon Theatre, Leicester Square, London in December, 1962 I believe this is still the greatest movie ever made. Everything comes together—script, directing, acting, design, editing, music. The audience is swept away by the immense scope of the film and certain images are burned in your mind forever.

The two men primarily responsible for bringing this together were the producer, Sam Spiegel and the director, David Lean. They have both been associated with wonderful films, separately and together, but they reached their pinnacle of achievement in "Lawrence."

Strangely enough, it almost didn't happen. David Lean told me once that he had sworn he would never work with Sam Spiegel again after "Bridge Over The River Kwai." Most producers are content to leave the creative side of film making to the director, involving themselves primarily with the business side, the script, major casting, daily trouble shooting and sometimes marketing. Spiegel, however, demanded a complete blueprint of the film, from storyboards to camera angles, to costumes, before one foot of film was shot. He was part of every single decision taken in its making.

David Lean was the most painstaking director I've ever come across. He could take years to put a motion picture together. Needless to say, these two ultimate perfectionists clashed frequently. "Kwai" had not been a happy experience for the director.

I asked him why he had decided to go back and work with Spiegel again.

"This was a film I really wanted to make. The story of this flawed hero set against the magnificent background of Arabia was too much of a challenge to pass up. I looked around at who was out there and saw that, despite his own flaws, Spiegel was the best producer in the world."

I spent a lot of time with Spiegel over the marketing life of this film and other films he produced for Columbia during the sixties. These included "The Chase", starring Marlon Brando and Robert Redford, in one of his first roles; "The Night of the Generals", which reunited Spiegel with Omar Sharif; "The Happening" and "The Swimmer", a strange tale starring Burt Lancaster.

Spiegel could be a difficult, demanding man at times with an intimidating presence. He also enjoyed his reputation as a womanizer. One of the more awkward moments I had with him was at the Brussels premiere of "Lawrence". It was a charity affair with young girls from Belgium's high society acting as hostesses. After Spiegel had been shown to his seat in the auditorium, Mike Frankovich, who at that time was head of Columbia's U.K. operation, took me to one side. He described one of the young hostesses.

"Sam liked the look of her. Go find her and see if she would like to join him for dinner afterwards. Make it clear that dinner is not all that is involved. If she would like money or a gift that will be okay."

I was taken aback. "I can't do that. These girls aren't hookers. They come from good families. I wouldn't even do this for myself, let alone someone else."

"Just do it," insisted Frankovich. "If she says no, you're off the hook. Look, nothing would happen anyway. Sam likes to be seen with young girls, but he's not up to it anymore." He walked away before I could respond.

Miserably, feeling like a pimp, I searched the lobby and other public areas of the vast downtown theater. I had no idea what I would do if I found her. I didn't see how I could do what I'd been asked. I know that many other publicists would have had no problems with such a task, but behind my extrovert, wise-cracking facade I was just a nervous kid from the suburbs.

Fortunately, all the hostesses had disappeared, presumably into the darkened auditorium. I tried half-heartedly to find her during the intermission but had no success.

There were no recriminations from Frankovich or Spiegel.

***

Peter O'Toole was another story. He certainly was up to it. He and Omar Sharif told me that they had an agreement with each other during the filming in North Africa and Spain. Whenever a female journalist visited the set, and there were a lot of them, they would take turns bedding them.

They thought of this as the luck of the draw. For instance, if it was O'Toole's turn and the visiting journalist was old or ugly or had a wooden leg he still had to go through with it. I was not told if there were any refusals.

When Peter came to Paris to promote the film I set up a schedule of press interviews at the Hotel Raphael, where he liked to stay. One of the first writers to show up was the famous Italian journalist, Oriana Fallaci who had previously met him during the filming of "Lawrence." I took her up to his suite. She was hardly in the room before she had pulled the pins out of her long, dark hair and was already starting to take her clothes off before I could make my exit.

O'Toole had another interview with a woman journalist at eleven the following morning. I tried calling his room when she arrived, but he didn't answer the phone. I went upstairs and persuaded the chambermaid to open the door. He was sound asleep—and alone. On the pillow next to him was a note from Oriana, which I read without shame.

"Thank you for a wonderful night," it said.

I shook Peter awake and told him about the reporter waiting downstairs. He assured me he would be there very quickly and he was. I didn't mention the note.

Over the next couple of days I felt like an air traffic controller, keeping the journalists in a holding pattern in the hotel bar while Peter O'Toole was being "interviewed" in his room.

I was amused at that time when friends, who had seen him in "Lawrence of Arabia" would insist that he was gay. Lawrence was an effete British army officer who enjoyed young Arab boys. Peter O'Toole is just a good actor.

He is also a good drinker, at least he was back then. One evening the two of us sat drinking scotch in the bar while he waited for his dinner companion. His date was late and I became stinking drunk. He didn't seem to be affected.

When I left the hotel I decided to walk round the Place de L'Etoile to clear my head. This is a huge plaza at the confluence of twelve broad avenues. The Arc de Triomphe sits in the center. It's a long walk. I didn't feel any better, so walked around it once more. I was still affected by the drink and by this time I was very hungry. I could have walked to any restaurant but got it into my head that I had to eat at a particular bistro on the left bank, the other side of town. Somehow I made it there through the frenetic Paris traffic and, of course, washed down my meal with a bottle of wine. I left the restaurant totally blitzed, but for the first time acted sensibly. I climbed into the back seat of my car and slept for four hours. When I woke up I was finally sober and felt like shit.

***

Alec Guinness was the antithesis of Peter O'Toole. He flew into London for the film's world premiere and I drove to the airport to pick him up. Modest and retiring, he was quite upset when I presented myself to him at the arrival gate.

"Dear boy, you came all the way out here to meet me! That really wasn't necessary. I could have taken a taxi," he said.

I haven't met too many stars with that attitude.

Take Richard Widmark. Please! He came to Paris to promote the film "The Long Boats," a Viking saga. We had booked him a room at the small but elegant Hotel de la Tremoille. The sole receptionist was talking on the phone when we arrived. He acknowledged our presence and indicated that he would be with us in a moment. For two minutes Widmark stamped his foot in ever growing impatience.

Finally, he roared, "I will not be treated this way," and stormed out of the hotel. I ran after him but he was adamant. There was no way he would stay at a hotel where he was treated so shabbily. He marched towards the nearby Plaza Athenee Hotel, a much larger, more famous and more expensive hotel. I had no choice but to return to the Tremoille and apologize to the receptionist. The scene that Widmark had made was, of course, just an excuse to change hotels.

***

"OLIVER!"

"Oliver!" the musical version of the Dickens story, released in 1968, is a delightful work. Directed by Sir Carol Reed, the film won six Oscars. It stars Ron Moody in the role of Fagin which he created on stage, Oliver Reed (no relation) as Bill Sykes and a 10-year-old Mark Lester in the title role.

I took Mark on a tour of several European countries to promote the film and found him to be a wonderfully spirited child. While on the trip he discovered that you can generate a minor electric shock through nylon carpeting. So, as soon as we arrived in a hotel he would start sliding his feet across the carpet to generate enough static electricity to give someone a shock—usually me. He also demanded that I tell him jokes continuously, which became difficult, as I didn't know too many jokes suitable for a 10-year-old. Nevertheless he was a levelheaded kid, unaffected by the fuss and attention.

As an infant he had been stricken by polio and doctors had told his family that he would be crippled all his life, but he had recovered. One blustery morning in Berlin, with snow dusting the streets, we took a car to the Olympic Stadium, scene of Hitler's 1936 Olympics. The place was empty but open. We found ourselves in the uppermost row of seats, looking down on the vast sunken arena. Mark asked if he could run a lap. I nodded. He trotted down the long aisle until he stood on the track. He looked up at me. I waved. Slowly he made his way round the circuit, a tiny figure dwarfed by this huge yet failed shrine to Aryan youth. He finished the tour and proudly climbed the steps to where I waited. A broad grin lit up his face. I hugged him. He had done something that not too many years earlier would have been thought impossible. I think he got more of a kick out of running that 400 meters lap than making "Oliver!" or any other movie.

There was another side to the Mark Lester story—his mother and father, the Parents from Hell. They were demanding and pushy and determined to milk their child's fame for all it was worth. At receptions and parties along the way, in Rome, Paris, Berlin and Vienna, they were the first to get to the food and the last to leave. They believed that if it was free they should take as much as they possibly could. They were forever wanting more money, more perks. They showed contempt for the other actors, particularly Jack Wild, a diminutive young man who had brilliantly portrayed the Artful Dodger. Their beautiful son was the only one who would amount to anything. He was a star for life. Of course, Mark never did make it and has long been out of acting.

One image from that tour stands out in my memory. Opera singer, Maria Callas was at the Vienna premiere. When I escorted Mark to his seat Miss Callas let out a yell.

"Oh, I must hold him. He is so beautiful," she cried. So, obediently, I lifted Mark up and hoisted him down the row of seats to where the great diva was sitting. She hugged him, kissed him and cooed over him until he could be passed back along the row. Mark took all of this with a quiet smile. I didn't ask him what he really thought about it all.

The only complaint I ever heard from Mark Lester was when he was describing his experience with Oliver Reed during the filming. Although he found the actor a pleasant enough man, "he was rough with me in the scenes we had together. He hurt me."

***

Oliver Reed hurt me too, but in a very different way. It happened in Zurich. He was the film's representative at the premiere, which was in aid of the Swiss Red Cross.

The day did not start well. It was one of those occasions that publicity executives have nightmares about. A press conference had been scheduled at our hotel for eleven in the morning. Nobody showed! Our local publicist had screwed up.

I figured the only way to handle the situation was to make a joke out of it. So I pretended to be a radio interviewer, using a bowl of olives as a microphone. To his credit, Oliver took it all in his stride. Besides, this gave us more drinking time and Oliver Reed made Peter O'Toole look like a teetotaler. Though I didn't realize it at the time I found out that Oliver made a hobby out of challenging people to drinking contests. He did it with great subtlety, easing his victim painlessly down the long road of perdition.

We did have a couple of journalists to interview over a long lunch, which was naturally a time of more drinking. At an afternoon reception the drinking continued.

We made our appearance at the theater for the start of the movie that evening, then slipped out to a bar next-door for the duration of the screening. Once the picture was over we were back at the theater for Oliver to gracefully accept the accolades. By this time we were beyond caring about split infinitives.

Some 30 people attended a resplendent post premiere dinner, all seated at one long table. The President of the Swiss Red Cross, who I believe was also President of the nation's Senate, was seated across from me. To my astonishment he started haranguing me in front of the entire gathering. He was complaining that Columbia Pictures had cheated him. Apparently, he felt that the charity had not received enough money from the theater takings. I had no idea what he was talking about, but promised to check into it. That didn't satisfy the man, who was determined to make a scene.

Down at the other end of the table, Oliver got involved. In a loud baritone voice he began singing "It's time we were leaving" to the tune of "O come all ye faithful."

Grateful for the diversion, I made my excuses, explaining that we had to catch a plane early in the morning. We left the President of the Swiss Senate grumbling to the person sitting next to him. I never heard any more about Columbia Pictures "cheating" the Red Cross.

Meanwhile, it was not yet midnight and Oliver had some serious drinking to do. At that time, and perhaps still today, Zurich wasn't a town that throbbed with excitement. The Swiss are a quiet people and their towns reflect that. However, a few well-placed inquiries led us to a private club and even got us in. Here we listened to music and talked. Oliver was a tough looking character and it wasn't all looks. He was part of that drinking, womanizing and fighting British actors' clique; people like Richard Burton, Robert Shaw, Richard Harris, Trevor Howard (see later story) and Peter O'Toole. Oliver carried a deep scar on his chin. He explained that it had been caused by a broken bottle during a pub brawl.

So we drank. By five we had been drinking with a reasonable amount of consistency for 18 hours. I think I had downed every alcoholic beverage known or unknown to man. I had not been particular whether it was wine or champagne, whisky or gin, cognac, crème de cacao or a mixture of all of the above. Some time before dawn I lifted a glass of something or other to my lips. I knew there was no way I could down it. I put it gently back on the table.

"Oliver, you win. I couldn't touch another drop," I said.

"Kiss my hand and call me King," he demanded.

He held out his hand imperiously. I kissed the back of it and said, "Thou art King!"

"Again!" he bellowed.

I repeated the ritual. "Thou art King!"

"Thank God," he moaned, falling forward, his head hitting the table.

The following morning I had the worst hangover of my life. I felt as if the Alps had dropped an avalanche right on my head.

At breakfast, Oliver was bright and cheerful, claiming that he had never had a hangover.

"You must drink this," he told me, handing me a glass of beer.

That was the last thing I wanted. The very thought made me want to throw up.

He insisted. "Hair of the dog."

Gingerly I took a sip, then a gulp, then slowly the entire glass. It stayed down and I really felt better. My headache was gone. I was almost human.

I did learn a lesson that day. I now drink in moderation and never mix my drinks.

Over the years, Oliver drank more and worked less. In the spring of 1999 he had a heart attack and died in a bar in Valetta on the island of Malta. He died in the way I'm sure he would have wanted to. He bought drinks for everyone in the bar, arm-wrestled sailors, knocked back 10 pints of beer and 12 glasses of rum and finally two glasses of whisky. The unpaid bar tab was $435. The King is dead. Long live the King!

***

As anyone who has read Dickens knows, the Artful Dodger is the archetype of all pickpockets, so it was ironic that Jack Wild, who played the Artful Dodger in the movie, should have his pocket picked in Paris. Well, not exactly his pocket. We were in a store buying some souvenirs and he put his wallet on the counter. In a moment it was gone. He should have known better.

Sir Carol Reed, who was also on that promotional trip to Paris, was a man with a wicked sense of humor. John Woolf, who produced "Oliver!" was terrified of flying and was in a very nervous state when I took them to Orly Airport for the trip back to London.

Sir Carol offered to buy him a beer. "It'll steady your nerves," he assured him. Sir Carol beckoned me over to the bar.

"Bring him his drink, but make sure you put the glass on this newspaper," he chortled. A headline screamed PLANE CRASHES: 125 KILLED.

"You wouldn't!" I said.

"Go on, do it."

So I did as the director asked. For a moment Woolf didn't see the paper. Then his face blanched.

"Oh, my God! Oh, my God!" he said.

I glanced over at Sir Carol who was still at the bar, a look of studied innocence on his face. Of course, they all made the brief flight to London without incident.

***

PETERS

Sir Carol Reed, funny though he could be, didn't make a living at it. This is a chapter about a couple of Peters who did. However, frequently people who are funny on stage or screen are shy or depressed in their private lives. Alec Guinness was a shy man who hid behind the characters he portrayed on the screen.

Peter Sellers was one of the funniest and cleverest comedic actors ever to grace the screen. During the last years of his life I laughed a lot with him and at him. He had a special mystique and yet he was a strange, tormented individual who had difficulty handling everyday chores.

I read recently that Blake Edwards, his "Pink Panther" director and writer, thought Sellers was a paranoid schizophrenic. I do know that he liked to talk to his mother a lot while on the set of his movies. She was dead at the time.

I met Peter Sellers for the first time at the Cannes Film Festival in 1979 when I worked for Lorimar Pictures. He was in town to promote "Being There", which was shortly going into production. It was based on the best selling book by Jerzy Kosinski.

I had organized a black tie dinner for 200 top international distributors at the Eden Roc restaurant at the Hotel du Cap in Cap d'Antibes. This most exclusive of restaurants is perched on a bluff overlooking the Mediterranean. Sellers was the guest of honor. As the dinner drew to a close, I went to his table and, sitting on top of a radiator, asked him if he wouldn't mind saying a few words to the distributors, who would hopefully be buying his film.

"No, if I go up there they'll expect me to do some schtick and I really don't want to do that," he said.

I told him that he only needed to say hello and thank them for showing up. He still demurred. I felt as if I were in the hot seat in more way than one.

At that point I nodded to Merv Adelson, chairman of Lorimar, who came over and asked Sellers the same thing. Me he could refuse. Merv was more difficult to turn down.

OF KINGS AND QUEENS AND MOVIE STARS

So Peter Sellers climbed on to the small stage and did 20 minutes of the funniest schtick I had ever heard. He explained the story of "Being There" in incomprehensible "Russian," leapt into his American salesman pitch, then became an upper class Englishman. My stomach ached from laughing.

Later, as he was leaving the restaurant, he grabbed a tray from a passing waiter, put a bottle of wine and two glasses on it and posed straight-faced next to a mural of a waiter holding a tray with a bottle of wine and two glasses. They looked like twins.

"We'll polish this off," he said to me. "You bastard! I saw you nod to Merv."

Peter Sellers was part of my personal cultural memory as I had grown up in England. While draining my first glass I reminded him of his start on BBC radio when he had a five minute "bit" in a variety program in which he did impersonations of stars. He called it Sellers' Market.

I think he got a kick out of my telling him that and, in fact, several months later released an album that he again called Sellers' Market. I don't know whether my memory jog inspired him to make the album, but it'd be nice to think so.

As brilliant as he was as a performer, Sellers was lost in the real world. Any practical arrangements, such as booking planes or hotels or restaurants had to be organized through his wife, Lynn Frederick. Lynn got a bad rap from Peter's family members after he died, but I had only positive experiences with her. She was very loving, protective and supportive.

Sellers returned to the Cannes Film Festival again in 1980 when "Being There" was in competition. In his role as Chance, the naive gardener who rose to a position of extreme power through a series of misunderstandings, Peter gave the performance of his life.

Just how important this part was to him is revealed in a story told me by Jerzy Kosinski. Jerzy received a call one day from a man who appeared very upset. He claimed "Being There" was based on his own life and he desperately needed to talk to the author. Jerzy was bewildered by the call because his work was pure fiction, but the man was so persuasive that he agreed to meet him for lunch. Coincidences do happen, thought Jerzy.

The man arrived on time for his appointment and, as he spoke, Jerzy was astonished to realize that indeed this was Chance in all his pure simplicity.

It was only when a little girl came up to his lunch companion and asked "Please Mr. Sellers, may I have your autograph?" that he realized who Chance really was. Sellers had read the book and was so taken with the character that he wanted to make the movie. He was aware that Kosinski had turned down all previous offers to film any of his books, so he hit on this subterfuge. Persuaded by Sellers' passion and interpretation of the character, Kosinski agreed to the production of the film, which was directed by Hal Ashby.

Peter Sellers, in his long and successful career, had never won an Oscar, nor any major acting award. This pained him greatly. By the time the 1980 Cannes Festival came around he was a very sick man, having survived more than one heart attack. He sensed that "Being There" would be his last chance so, against his doctors' wishes, he left his hospital bed in Ireland to fly to Nice for the circus at nearby Cannes.

He had been told by a number of people, including myself, that he was a shoo-in for the Best Actor Palmares. Usually actors and directors will remain at the festival for the three or four days surrounding the screening of their film, then leave, but Peter arrived at the beginning of the festival and stayed until the very end. He wasn't going to miss this opportunity to collect his one and only trophy.

At Lorimar we didn't want to repeat the previous year's dinner at Eden Roc, so we gave a party in the garden of a Lebanese restaurant, just behind the Croisette, Cannes' main drag. Sellers and Kosinski were representing "Being There" at the party together with producer, Andrew Braunsberg. In addition we had "The Big Red One" in competition and, in town to plug that film were writer/director, Sam Fuller, who gave more than 50 separate interviews (more about Sam later), producer Gene Corman and stars Robert Carradine, Kelly Ward and Bobby DiCicco. I believe this was the first time that a production company (not a major studio) had two films in competition in Cannes.

Robert Kaylor presented his film "Carny" in the Directors Fortnight sidebar event. Jodie Foster was the star. Ralph Waite was also there to promote his wonderful little film, "On the Nickel", which was being premiered in the market.

In all, I had a dozen celebrities to look after.

OF KINGS AND QUEENS AND MOVIE STARS 49

The garden party was a hot ticket and we had carefully selected the media who would attend. Nevertheless, one rather large, sweaty American photographer and well-known gatecrasher, who was not on the list, demanded to be allowed in. When the girl at the gate refused, he hit her. Enraged, I grabbed the man and threw him against a car parked in the street. We were separated before I could really hurt him. Who am I kidding! He'd have beaten the crap out of me. As it was, he went around town telling people that he would kill me. I complained to the festival press office and was able to have his accreditation withdrawn. As they say in Hollywood, he'll never work in this town again.

On the day of the party, Jerzy Kosinski got the news that he had been invited to make his acting debut in Warren Beatty's "Reds". Jerzy was ecstatic.

"Leonard, next time I see you I will ignore you. I will be a famous movie star," he joked. In fact, he gave a credible performance in "Reds".

During his three days in Cannes, Jerzy worked hard, giving more than 20 press interviews. I found him a fascinating, larger than life character whose exhilarating disposition gave me no clue of his intentions to take his own life. His suicide a number of years later made me immensely sad.

Peter Sellers made it to the official press conference on the morning his film was shown in competition, but because of his illness I had to twice postpone a television press conference to be held at the Carlton Hotel. On the third try he was well enough to be driven in from the Hotel Du Cap, 40 minutes outside town. He performed for the dozen or so television crews who had been waiting patiently, then returned to his hotel.

On the Monday morning, which was the final day of the festival, I attended a press conference at the Palais du Festival. It was announced that the best actor award had gone to Frenchman, Michel Piccoli for a role in which his own voice was not even used. The film was Italian and an anonymous Italian actor had dubbed in his voice. The production company, Gaumont, was very influential at the Cannes Festival. In other words, it looked very much as if the fix was in and Peter Sellers had been screwed.

I walked across the street back to my office and, with a heavy heart, called Sellers at his hotel to give him the bad news. While I was talking to him a British journalist who had followed me from the Palais, asked if I was talking to Sellers. When I said that I was, he requested an interview. Lousy timing.

At the beginning of the festival Sellers had told me that under no circumstances did he want to talk to this journalist. At one time they had been friends, but at last year's festival this man had written an article about Sellers' alleged marital problems. Peter had blamed that article for almost ruining his marriage. Like I said—lousy timing.

Nevertheless, I felt I had to pass on the request.

"Of course I'll meet him," said Peter, to my astonishment. "Have him come over to the Hotel du Cap. I'll be waiting in the restaurant—with a tureen of hot soup which I will empty over him."

There was no interview.

That afternoon Peter and Lynn Sellers flew to England on a private plane.

Three months later, I was sitting in a Hollywood screening room watching a rough cut of the film "S.O.B." with its director, Blake Edward and with Henry Mancini, who would be composing the music, when word came that Sellers had had another heart attack. We were all in shock. Mancini was, of course, the composer of the Peter Sellers "Pink Panther" movies which were directed by Edwards. That evening, Lynn Frederick flew from Los Angeles to London to be with her husband. Peter died the next day.

**

Sellers was not the only British comedic talent bearing the first name Peter. I am referring to Peter Ustinov who was, of course, far more than a comedic talent. He was an actor, raconteur, writer, director, producer, cartoonist, wit and tennis player, but when I had lunch with him at Les Ambassadeurs in London in 1961 I discovered another, hidden talent.

We were with the famous British journalist, Nancy Spain, who was interviewing him about his film "Romanoff and Juliet". Polyglot Ustinov was in fine form, flitting from French to Russian with the waiters and anyone else in earshot.

I mentioned how much I had liked the music in the film, particularly the waltz theme.

"Glad you liked it," he said. "I wrote it myself, sort of." He explained

OF KINGS AND QUEENS AND MOVIE STARS

that he had been playing around with the fast march theme, changed the tempo and, presto, had a whole new piece of music. He then proceeded to amuse everyone in the restaurant by playing it, using his voice to imitate every instrument in the orchestra, miming the violin, trumpet, saxophone, drums etc.

A few years later I bumped into him on the Champs Elysees in Paris. I happened to be with a beautiful Bengali girl, Zaharat Anam, exotically dressed in a gold sari and bejeweled hair. Now this girl was someone special. I had met her at Copenhagen Airport, on my way home to Paris. She was going some place else, but told me she would be in Paris in a couple of weeks. I asked her to give me a call when she got into town. She did and caused a sensation wherever we went. Walking down the street we were followed by a line of men, stunned by her beauty. One man fell off his chair at a sidewalk café, straining to get a better look. When I told a colleague at Columbia Pictures about this girl he thought I was exaggerating and agreed to go on a double date to see this wondrous creature for himself. As we walked into the restaurant the following evening the musicians who had been playing suddenly forgot their music and stopped playing in the middle of a number. A waiter crossing the dance floor looked up and dropped the dishes he was carrying. The girl, who had been living in California, told me that she had been dating Marlon Brando. I had no reason to disbelieve her, knowing his predilection for the exotic.

Peter Ustinov deserted a circle of friends who were roaring with laughter when he spotted me on the street. He elbowed his way through his cordon of admirers and regaled us right there on the sidewalk with one story after another for almost an hour—without once taking his eyes off her.

What am I, I thought. Chopped liver?

At one point I realized someone was trying to attract my attention. I saw an old friend, from my teenage days in London, waiting to be noticed. I motioned that I had noticed him and after a while beckoned him over. He glided right past me, hand outstretched to Peter. I stood there, mouth agape, feeling like that towering bowl of chopped liver.

"Oh, Mr. Ustinov, what a pleasure to meet you in the flesh," he said with a nervous laugh.

Okay, so it was childish, but I got a kick out of that meeting. My bland suburban past had caught up with my exciting, jet-set present.

In the late eighties, I met Peter Ustinov again. We were at the Cannes Film Festival and he had just attended a luncheon with Prince Charles and Princess Diana, a luncheon where he had not been served any food. He had returned to his hotel, the Martinez, and was sitting at a pool side table, having finally ordered something to eat, when I happened by.

"Hello," I said brightly. "How are you, Peter?"

I guess he was like me. Being hungry puts me in a lousy mood. He grumbled about the mixed pleasures of dining with royalty. "Right now I don't want to talk. I just want to eat," he said. I took the broad hint and left.

But that encounter was a mere blip on the serene continuum of life. If you want trouble you go to the mistress of mayhem, the expert in ego—Barbra Streisand...

***

BARBRA

"Funny Girl" was due to open in Paris and I don't recall such anticipation for any film before or since. The picture had premiered in New York in September of 1968 and now, a few months later, it was France's turn. It still amazes me how word gets out. Nobody had seen Barbra Streisand perform and, at this stage in her career, few had bought her albums, yet everyone seemed to know that this was the birth of a great star.

Columbia Pictures had taken over the magnificent Paris Opera House for the premiere. We had even rented an entire Metro subway train to take our V.I.P. guests to the Gare de l'Opera, a short walk to the Opera House entrance. We had engaged the services of Georges Cravenne, a brilliant special events organizer.

On the big night everything went like clockwork—at first. The guests arrived on time, Les Gardes Republicaine lined the splendid curved staircase in their plumed helmets, their polished cuirasses gleaming in the television lights. At the head of the stairs stood Leon Citron, France's pre-eminent television anchor, who would be interviewing Streisand live for the evening news.

We had held several meetings in the weeks preceding the event trying to come up with one really big idea to grab the headlines. The most obvious idea was to ask her co-star, Omar Sharif, to escort her to the theater, but their affair, which had flourished briefly while "Funny Girl" was being filmed, was over. Besides, even though Sharif would be there, this did not seem a particularly brilliant idea.

I suggested asking Maurice Chevalier, France's greatest living musical star, to accompany Streisand, America's newest musical star, to the theater. He was asked and accepted. Wonderful!

A junior member of our staff was assigned to go in the limo to Chevalier's home and from there drive to Streisand's hotel.

As I have already stated, everything went like clockwork—except...

The limousine carrying Streisand, Chevalier and our publicist arrived outside the Opera House exactly on time. The honor guard was ready, the photographers, the cameramen, Leon Citron, everyone was ready.

Barbra Streisand however, had different ideas. She ordered the limo driver to go around the block a few times. She was going to keep them waiting. She was going to make an entrance. After all, she was a Big Star. She kept that car going for another 20 minutes. Our inexperienced publicist didn't have the clout to countermand her orders. Perhaps no one would have. Barbra is not an easy lady to go against.

The television network producer was demanding to know what was going on and Citron was having a fit. The rest of us weren't much better. We couldn't understand what the delay was.

Eventually they arrived, arm in arm, brilliant smiles on their faces. The impatient photographers and curious guests who had not taken their seats, rushed them. The crush of people was enormous. They could make no headway. The familiar charming smile on Chevalier's face froze into a grimace of fear.

I was watching the drama unfold from the upper level of the vast lobby. I rushed down through the throng, pushing people aside so that I could get in front of them and help make a path. It took us 25 minutes to get through the lobby and up the stairs. As the phalanx of photographers and onlookers drew level with Leon Citron he was swept aside, loudly protesting that he was on live television and had to have his interview. It didn't happen. At the door of the auditorium one particularly persistent photographer refused to budge. I shoved his arm away impatiently and his camera hit his nose, sending blood gushing down his face.

Finally everyone was seated and the film started—45 minutes late.

The following morning Streisand was scheduled to give a press conference for a large group of international journalists we had invited from all over Europe. As most of them had planes to catch, we held this conference separately. The French would get to her in the afternoon.

British, German, Italian and Dutch reporters and journalists from every country in Western Europe waited in the hotel ballroom. The minutes ticked by. No Barbra Streisand. She was doing it again!

I asked her manager where the hell she was.

He shrugged his shoulders indifferently.

Two hours later she wandered in, as if nothing had happened. I asked her where she had been.

"I went shopping," she said casually.

"Didn't you realize that you had a press conference? Journalists are here from all over Europe. They have planes to catch."

She simply smiled. All this fuss was obviously beneath her.

Fuming, I escorted her to the ballroom.

Most of the press had already left. Those who remained were in lousy moods. She smiled sweetly at their complaints and answered all their questions.

I think Barbra knew exactly what she was doing. Even at this early stage in her career she knew how to get attention. She had a keen nose for publicity.

Whatever the reason, the movie was a hit all over Europe.

***

MOSCOW

In 1967, the United States of America and the Soviet Union were still embroiled in the Cold War. Paranoid suspicion was equally balanced on both sides of the Iron Curtain. It was therefore a breakthrough almost on a par with Nixon's ping-pong mission to China, when America decided to send its largest ever contingent to that summer's Moscow Film Festival. More than 60 actors, directors, producers, studio executives, officials, journalists and one publicist—me, attended.

The entire contingent was briefed by the United States Ambassador on the dangers of wandering around Moscow. Agents provocateur were on every street corner and they were likely to offer to buy our dollars on the black market or ball point pens or jeans. Under no circumstances, we were instructed, were we to accept their offers or blandishments. We were told to assume that every Russian who came in contact with us, particularly if they spoke English, was a spy. We were warned that many of the hotel rooms were bugged. Just keep your noses clean and you'll be all right.

Oh, boy!

My own problems started right away. You don't know the meaning of red tape until you go through it in Red Square. Although my visa was in order, somehow the room that was reserved for me was not available. After many agonizing hours of being interrogated by the KGB, and only with the personal intervention of Jack Valenti, who headed up the Motion Picture Association of America and who led the American delegation, was I saved from Lubianka prison. Jack twisted arms and got me a room in his hotel.

Actually, he found me more than a room. It was a suite located in the huge, newly built, Hotel Rossia. The suite was being held for Mo Rothman, who was not expected for a few days. By the time he arrived they would have a regular room for me.

As I was in a V.I.P. suite, bugs were almost certainly lurking in light fixtures, air ducts or behind pictures. Curious, I searched but found nothing.

OF KINGS AND QUEENS AND MOVIE STARS

My initial belief was that all this phobic behavior was part of the "commie under every bed" attitude I had encountered with certain Americans. A series of incidents quickly made a believer out of me.

One of the American films scheduled to be shown was "Young Americans," a documentary about an idealistic and ethnically diverse young people's choir that toured the country. Innocent enough, right?

Not by the festival organizers' standards it wasn't. They considered it blatant American propaganda and rejected the film.

The film's producer, Robert Cohn, went nuts. He demanded that I draft a letter to be telexed to the State Department in Washington. He gave me the gist of what he wanted said and left me to work on it while he went to lunch. Unfortunately, this whole conversation took place in front of the woman who had been given to the American delegation to assist us, a woman who was obviously spying.

Feeling her eyes boring in the back of my head, I valiantly typed away. I was convinced this whole thing was a waste of time.

After I had finished the letter, I slipped it in my pocket and went for a walk down Gorky Street. I had this horrible feeling that I was being followed and was waiting to feel an official hand on my shoulder any minute. I arrived at a small park and sat down on a bench, casually looking around. I saw no one suspicious so I stood up and retraced my steps to the hotel.

I gave Robert Cohn the letter, happy to have it out of my possession. It was duly sent to the State Department, but absolutely nothing came out of it and the film was never shown, to Jack's considerable fury. I guess I can't blame him. His trip to the Soviet Union had been a complete waste of time.

One of the problems of being in the Soviet Union back in the sixties was that you couldn't buy a Western newspaper or see anything but Russian propaganda on television, that is if you could understand it, so those of us who were news nuts were freaking out. The embassy came up with a solution. Every day they Xeroxed a sheet of items taken from the news wires received at the embassy. Teenage children of embassy officials were given the job of going from room to room at the Hotel Rossia, where we were all staying, and pushing these sheets under the doors.

One of the rooms had been vacated by the American who was supposed to be there, and a Russian was in the room. For a Russian to be able to stay at that hotel at that time he had to have the right connections. This one did. No sooner had the kid, a 14 year-old-girl, pushed the sheet under the door than it was flung open and the four KGB operatives inside grabbed her and dragged her into the room, slamming the door behind her. They interrogated the terrified child for four hours, accusing her of dispersing American propaganda; no matter that her father was a diplomat. Eventually he was called and the girl was allowed to go free.

One of the American trade journalists covering the festival was gay and he had made the mistake of bringing his Cuban lover with him on the trip. One night, the man was kidnapped by a group of Cuban agents who were free to do their own policing on the streets of Moscow. The man was beaten and tortured until he managed to escape. He returned to the hotel and hid in his room for several days waiting to get a flight out. I learned of this at lunch one day. The journalist was taking extra apples and rolls and putting them in his pocket. When I asked him why, he explained that his friend couldn't leave their room for fear of being captured again.

He really wasn't missing much at mealtimes. The Russians had never heard the word "service" at that time so it could take you several hours to get through a meal of stringy chicken and tasteless vegetables.

The 1967 Moscow Film Festival was not all doom and gloom however and one night was particularly enjoyable.

Russia did not have such decadent bourgeois establishments as night clubs at this time, but in recognition of their international visitors they did open a club for the duration of the festival on the top floor of the Hotel Moskva. This was a good walk across Red Square from the Hotel Rossia and on this particular evening my date was a young American television actress. When we arrived the place was swinging, with a Russian jazz band playing and the vodka and caviar flowing.

At one point everyone stopped talking and turned to watch the band. Even servants timorously peered through the kitchen doors in wonderment at this new sound. Sitting in with the band was one of the great jazz musicians of all time—baritone saxophone player, Gerry Mulligan. He was at the festival with his wife, Sandy Dennis, star of "Up The Down Staircase", which was being screened in competition. His music was so great that it elevated the local musicians into playing better than they had ever played before. I'll never forget the excitement of that sound.

My date and I, meanwhile, had fallen in with a group of soulful Georgian theater exhibitors. Russians, and that includes Georgians in this instance, like to sing when they are drunk and, with the several bottles of Georgian brandy they and we had downed, singing was definitely on the agenda. We decided that everyone should sing a folk song from their country, so we heard beautiful Russian, Georgian, American and Italian songs and then when it was my turn, "Irish Eyes Are Smiling". I had never been to Ireland, had no Irish blood, but it was all I could think of at the time.

As my date and I walked across Red Square, on our way back to our hotel, the bells of St. Basil struck the hour. It was 4:00 a.m. and we watched the changing of the guard in front of Lenin's tomb. It was all very romantic. On an impulse, I swept her into my arms, bent her low over my knees, as if we had been dancing the tango, and kissed her passionately on the lips.

A police whistle blew precisely one inch from my right ear and, right there, I broke the world record for a standing jump. When I landed, I turned round and saw two policemen standing there. What law had we broken? Would I, despite it all, soon find out what the inside of a gulag looked like? The two officers looked at us sternly for a moment, and then burst out laughing. They had just been having fun with a couple of unsuspecting foreigners. They walked away, shaking their heads with glee at the joke they had pulled on us.

Still shaking, we quickly finished our walk to the hotel. She suggested I spend what was left of the night in her room. I wasn't sure that this was a good idea when I saw that the dezhurnaya, the elderly woman who kept the keys for that floor, was stationed right outside her door. We all knew that the Russians were very moralistic in matters such as this.

The girl didn't think it would be a problem. She was gorgeous and willing so I overcame my fears and followed her into the room. A few short hours later, I left and there was the babushka still seated at her table. She gave me a knowing wink and smiled. All was well with the world.

After two weeks in Russia we were all glad to board the plane home. As we took off, I felt as if a great weight had been removed from my shoulders. I had always believed that the Communist bogeyman was just a fabrication of American propaganda. After those two weeks I knew it was more than that—and also less. My entanglements with officials had been frightening, but encounters with ordinary people had been refreshing and disarming.

***

My second visit to Moscow in 1971 (see "Honeymoons"), again as the delegation's publicist, also had a political undercurrent, though the atmosphere had eased considerably. The leader of our delegation was Bruce Herschensohn, at this time head of the USIA, later an aide to Richard Nixon, in his final tumultuous days as President, and more recently U.S. senatorial candidate in California. Bruce was a pleasant enough man but his judgment was marred by right-wing blinkers. At that time he saw everything as a communist plot against the good old USofA.

One of the films being shown at the festival was a British documentary about the Vietnam war. The filmmaker was a well known Communist, so the film, obviously, gave a North Vietnamese slant to the war.

Now this really pissed Bruce off. He told me that he wanted to lodge a complaint with the festival and would threaten to withdraw American movies. I counseled him to keep quiet.

"If you say nothing, the film will just disappear among all the others showing here. It's only a documentary, not a major epic. If you make a fuss you will be falling right into their hands, giving them the publicity they crave," I told him with what I thought was great wisdom.

He didn't go for it. Instead, he lodged an official complaint.

Now it was the turn of the Russians to get angry and I can't say I blame them. They wanted nothing to do with the Americans and made all sorts of dire threats of their own. I was the only member of the American delegation they would talk to. After several separate meetings with Herschensohn and the festival authorities I was finally able to smooth things over and avert a nasty, and totally unnecessary international incident.

As I had warned Herschensohn, the fuss gave the documentary maker all the publicity he craved.

Smooth talking was not always the most effective way to get things done.

I had arrived in Moscow a few days early to make sure that the posters

OF KINGS AND QUEENS AND MOVIE STARS   61

of the films we were showing were put on display. Somehow the Czech, the Polish, the East German and even the Indian displays were up, but the Americans kept being shunted to one side. Finally, on the opening day, I lost my patience. The displays were being assembled in a large room in the basement of our hotel. I walked to the head of the stairs and started yelling at the workers in every language I knew, using every abusive word I could think of. They didn't understand a word I said, but certainly understood the tone. Within two hours we had all our posters in place.

That year I was probably the only person to be a member of two delegations. As I worked for Columbia Pictures I was naturally with the Americans. Because I was born in England and speak with a British accent, the sparse British delegation asked me to join them. But I am a publicist and wise to the ways of the world. The real reason was that they wanted to get close to me to hit me up for a favor. They knew that Leslie Caron, one of the few international celebrities attending the festival, was a friend of mine. The English had been invited to lunch by the festival authorities and wanted a bit of glamour to spruce up the occasion and make them look good. Leslie agreed to join me for lunch with them. We discovered that the Russian idea of lunch was a long series of vodka toasts and a few pieces of chocolate candy.

The head of the British delegation, Andy Workman, decided to tell a joke about a film director who went to heaven. It was a long tale, made interminable by the constant interruption of the translator.

Leslie and I rejoiced when the epic finally came to an end, only to have our hopes of escape dashed when the head of the Soviet delegation rose to tell <u>his</u> story of a director who went to heaven.

By this time it was well past the normal lunch hour and all we had had was a little chocolate and a lot of vodka. The joke, now interrupted by its English translation, was so unfunny that we found it hilarious. Influenced no doubt by the vodka sloshing around inside us, we laughed until our sides hurt.

***

SEX IN HAMBURG AND OTHER GERMAN DELIGHTS

When Columbia Pictures planned the release of the adventure story, "Mackenna's Gold" in 1969 I decided to make a major effort. I leased a Boeing 727 to take all the stars, with the exception of Gregory Peck, on a tour of Europe. Omar Sharif, Telly Savalas, Eli Wallach (with his wife Ann Jackson) and Ted Cassidy, who had played "Lurch" in the Addams Family television series, made the trip, which covered a number of countries.

Most of the group were sophisticated, seasoned world travelers, but Cassidy had barely been outside his native Texas, let alone the United States, and was totally bewildered by the strange sights, sounds and smells of Europe. Because he was so lost, my compassionate side took hold and I found myself spending more time with him than all the other actors together, even though they were of greater publicity value. At breakfast in our Rome hotel one morning he was confronted by the mystery of a soft-boiled egg in its shell. Apparently they don't serve eggs that way in Texas.

"How do I eat this thing?" he whispered to me in embarrassment. He was as grateful as a heifer being freed from a thorny thicket when I showed him how it was done. Cassidy, a giant of a man, was really a child, unabashedly thrilled by all that he saw. Most stars accept a publicist's hard work on their behalf as their given due. Ted, who was ill-at-ease with the trappings of stardom, was not like that. One afternoon while still in Rome he ventured out by himself and bought me a silk tie. It was an unexpected and sweet gesture.

The final stop was Hamburg. By the time we got there, Omar and Telly had perfected a comedy routine which they performed on the stage before the showing of the film. They had a great time and the audience loved it.

After the screening we were all invited to an exclusive party at the home of a local prince. They have a lot of those in Germany. The place was magnificent. The wood-paneled rooms were covered with paintings by every major European artist, discreetly lit by baby spots hidden in elaborate ceiling moldings.

OF KINGS AND QUEENS AND MOVIE STARS

As we stood in line for the buffet style meal, making polite conversation with Hamburg's society leaders, a reporter from Bild Zeitung, Germany's highest circulation newspaper, whispered in my ear.

"This is boring isn't it? Now, if you want I can show you all a really good time." He sounded like a pimp offering the services of his girls—which wasn't too far from the truth.

The journalist explained that there was a club near the infamous Reeperbahn where we could see things that would blow our minds—and other things! However, these "events" would not occur if any women went along. It would have to be a stag night.

I asked our actors if they were interested in taking this detour. Omar and Telly were, so after the reporter had called to alert the club that we were on our way, a small group of us made our excuses and took off for the Triangle Club, an establishment which still exists today.

As we walked through the door of the dimly lit club we were greeted by a beautiful hostess dressed in a magnificent white evening gown.

"Welcome to the Triangle Club," she said. At that precise moment her lovely gown fell to the floor, leaving her completely naked.

"Oh my, how embarrassing! My clothes seem to have fallen off," she said, straight-faced.

We were shown to our seats at the base of a raised stage in the center of the room. A nude girl stepped in front of us and proceeded to display a unique use for a bottle of Vat 69. She was joined by another girl and no longer needed the whisky bottle. We watched a series of sexual performances with the two girls, a girl and a man and even members of the audience joining in, aided by ribald comments from the spectators.

I stole a look at Omar Sharif who was seated to my left. His face was creased in a beatific smile. I did a double take when I saw one of the hostesses on her knees between us. She was deeply engrossed.

When we left the Triangle Club the Bild Zeitung reporter suggested we might like to visit the Herbertstrasse, Hamburg's red light street. Only Omar agreed, insisting, although I was dead on my feet, that I come with him. So I tagged along with the reporter and his photographer. When the latter tried to take a picture of Omar I told him to put his camera away.

"Come on. We're here as friends. This isn't a story," I said.

Chagrined, he explained that it was just force of habit.

It was a cold winter night, with flurries of snow falling and a layer of slush clinging to the sidewalk. Herbertstrasse is one block of row houses with barricades at either end to stop casual passers-by seeing something that might offend them. A large sign on the barricades announced that juveniles were not permitted.

Women of all kinds sat in windows or stood in doorways. As we passed one overweight, over-age blonde seated at a second floor window, Omar stopped.

"There's one of my fans. I do believe she wants my autograph. Let's go," he said, grabbing me by the arm. Pulling my arm out of his grasp, I looked up at the window and told him that this is where I drew the line.

Omar shrugged and waved at the hooker. She disappeared from the window as he climbed the four steps into the house.

The two journalists and I waited outside, stamping our feet and slapping our hands against our bodies to keep warm.

"Look, this is ridiculous," I said. "We're freezing our buns off here. Let's go inside and see if we can get a cup of coffee from some of the other girls."

Sure enough, the two other girls in the house were only too glad of our company. They closed the blinds to indicate that they were "busy" and pulled their best china from a top shelf in the kitchen.

Eventually, Omar came down the stairs, straightening his tie. His companion followed, preening herself and saying that she had just had "the most beautiful man in the world."

We all sat around that kitchen table for hours, drinking coffee and listening to the girls' fascinating stories about their pimps and strange johns.

Dawn was starting to silhouette the city skyline as we left. I paid the girls for their coffee and time. I think it was about 250DM ($125).

Later, Omar told me that he loved talking to and listening to prostitutes. They could tell the most incredible stories. I had to agree with him. I just wish I could recall the details of their conversation that night. Their tales would have filled a book by themselves.

When I returned to Paris I prepared my expenses as usual. Being a

OF KINGS AND QUEENS AND MOVIE STARS 65

reasonably honest person, I entered the expenditure of 250DM as "coffee in brothel." I was curious to see the reaction from New York. Reaction was zero. My expenses were approved without comment.

***

At the time of the preceding adventure I knew Germany well, having lived there in 1966 and 1967, traveling throughout the country, supervising Columbia's German and Austrian advertising, publicity and promotions during those two years. It was an interesting but not particularly enjoyable period of my life.

When I was first asked to move from Paris to Munich I declined. My grandmother, uncles, aunts and cousins had died in the holocaust; shot in the street or gassed in concentration camps. I was not going to live among the people who had done this. It was, however, made clear to me that this was not a request.

"Besides," said Marion Jordan, one of my bosses, "think of all those gorgeous German broads waiting to leap into bed with you." I was single at the time.

Despite Marion's description of my future life, I made the move with heavy heart and much trepidation. Those two years in Germany were not easy. I personally witnessed only a couple of instances of anti-Semitism yet it was hard to make friends. My German became fluent. I joined a tennis club, but I remained a stranger in a strange land, even though I think of myself as an easy-going guy.

Having lived through the Second World War, I sometimes found the situation downright weird. The general manager of Columbia Pictures in Germany, Erich Müller, was a Panzer captain in World War II who fought to the suburbs of Moscow. His sales manager was one of Germany's most decorated paratroopers. I liked them both. They didn't choose the country they were born in.

My modern Munich apartment faced on to the Schuttberg, a beautiful, hilly park built on the rubble caused by allied bombs. My own brother had flown one of those bombers. I did an oil painting of that park and it still hangs in my home.

In local elections held while I was living in Bavaria one out of 12 voted for the neo-Nazi party. I would frequently visit the beer hall in which Hitler had plotted his kampf. I would look around and I knew that many of his former followers were in that same room. I felt a little guilty for being there.

Though I spent most of those two years scheming to get back to Paris, there were some amusing times.

One of my haunts was the bar of the Bayerische Hof, one of the two top hotels in Munich at that time. It did not have the pretentiousness of the Vierjahreszeiten, the other major hotel, and had more of an old Bavarian feel to it. From the oak-lined bar you could survey the hotel lobby. For a couple of hours in the early evening it also served as the headquarters of the city's leading newspaper columnist so, if you were a publicist with a story to plant, that was the place to be.

One evening, after my journalist friend had left, I was sitting by myself with only a glass of beer for company. A lovely, long-limbed blonde in her mid twenties was sitting a couple of tables away and we made eye contact. I came up with the totally original idea of offering to buy her a drink. She accepted and before long we had moved to a nearby restaurant for dinner. The girl invited me into her apartment "for coffee." It was a large, high-ceilinged place with paintings covering every wall.

We sat close together on her couch but when I tried to kiss her she stopped me.

"If you want to spend the night with me you must buy one of my paintings," she said softly.

I looked at her in astonishment.

"You're a hooker?"

"I'm an artist with very little money and this is the only way I can sell my paintings," she replied.

I looked around the room. It was obvious that no two paintings were done by the same artist. They couldn't be her own work.

I no longer recall the price she was asking, but I do remember that it wasn't very much and I could certainly afford it. However, my macho ego told me that I should never pay to sleep with a woman, even in this indirect manner. Buying her dinner didn't count.

I kissed her chastely on the cheek, took one last sad look at her high four-poster bed, and left.

I was hardly out of her apartment building when I started to regret my action. Some of those paintings weren't bad and what a wonderful conversation piece my art treasure would have been, to say nothing of that missed night of pleasure.

The following evening I was back in the Bayerische Hof bar, hoping to find her there and wanting to tell her that I had changed my mind. She didn't show, but another woman was sitting at the same table. She wore an elegant, low-cut gown, was in her late thirties and a real knock-out. Once again I found myself looking into a strange woman's eyes. She smiled encouragement, but I couldn't bring myself to talk to her. I didn't want to end up with a whore, even a beautiful whore. After about half an hour of this she sighed, stood up and walked out of the room.

I asked the bartender, Herr Zimmerman, if he knew who she was.

"The Countess? Oh yes, she always stays here when she is in Munich."

***

SPACESHIPS IN MEXICO

One morning in April of 1983 I quit CBS Theatrical Films. Two hours later Universal asked me to coordinate the world-wide marketing of David Lynch's "Dune."

Frank Herbert's classic science fiction epic, with all the inventiveness and complexities of its fictitious planets, its many layered society of a distant future dealing with politics, religion and ecology, had been my favorite book for many years. Now I was being asked to become involved in it myself!

I recall that all this happened one Tuesday. Charles Glenn, who headed up worldwide marketing for Universal Studios, had heard that I was looking for a job. Once I was in his office he told me to close the door and said he would not allow me to leave until I had agreed to work on the film. Sweet words!

Four days later I was on a plane to Mexico City where filming on "Dune" had started, following a year of pre-production planning and a total of six years in development.

Fred Skidmore, head of domestic publicity at Universal (it was he who had recommended me for the job), and I were to have dinner that first evening with Ronnie Chasen who headed up the motion picture division at Rogers & Cowan. This large public relations agency had been engaged to work on the film. It was not the first time Ronnie and I had crossed paths—or swords. I had fired her from the CBS account a year previously. I asked Fred not to tell her I was there. I just wanted to see her face. Sure enough, when she showed up in the lobby of the Camino Real Hotel her face blanched and her mouth fell open.

"Wha, what does CBS have to do with 'Dune?" she stammered.

"Nothing," I replied. "I'm with Universal now, coordinating everything on the film, including P.R."

"Oh, how nice," she said, with a total lack of conviction.

The following day we were all driven to Churubusco Studios to meet with executive producer Dino De Laurentiis, his daughter Raffaella, who

OF KINGS AND QUEENS AND MOVIE STARS 69

was the producer, and the unit publicist, Anne Strick, a wonderfully warm and intelligent person.

That day we started to map out the most extensive marketing campaign in the history of Universal Studios at that point, a campaign as complex as the movie itself. I had to cover publicity, advertising, promotions, music, publishing and licensing.

The film was shot on eight sound stages at Churubusco where 75 sets were put together—from a series of "underground" passages to a magnificent palace. A crew of 700 built sets, furniture, costumes and some of them even spent three months cleaning up a section of the Samalayuca Desert near Juarez so that it would look like the arid planet Arrakis. With 21 speaking roles and 10,000 extras this was an enormous undertaking.

The director David Lynch is a fascinating character. He came to "Dune" fresh from his success with "Elephant Man," but would be the first to admit that he had taken on a tad too much with "Dune." Nevertheless, despite all the chaos around him, David always appeared calm. Whenever I saw him he was dressed the same way—white shirt buttoned at the throat, no tie, black jacket. Twice a day he disappeared for 20 minutes of meditation.

I once asked this polite, clean-cut, All American guy how come his films always had gruesome scenes and horribly deformed people.

"Isn't it better to act out my fantasies on the screen than in real life?" was his response.

One of his most unpleasant looking creations was the evil Baron Harkonnen, portrayed by Kenneth McMillan. As I was having lunch in the commissary one day McMillan showed up in full make-up. His face was covered in vile yellow boils.

"Aghh, you look horrible," I said.

"Come here and give us a kiss," he joked, offering the side of his face to my lips. "They're all loaded, too," he added.

He was about to do a scene where a doctor would lance those boils. By 'loaded' he indicated that the boils were already filled with "pus."

I declined his offer politely.

Kyle MacLachlan, the then unknown actor who portrayed the lead character, Paul Atreides, told me that he had read "Dune" as a youngster and was so overwhelmed by the book that he had actually convinced himself he was the reincarnation of Paul Atreides. It seemed, therefore, a natural turn of fate that he would be asked to play the role.

Sting, the English rock star, played the Baron's nephew, Feyd. I don't think he was too happy being there. On a day when we were not shooting I was sitting by the pool at the Hotel Camino Real, when he walked by with a tennis racket in his hand. I am something of a tennis nut myself and rarely travel without a racket —just in case.

"Hi, I see you're a tennis player. Want to play some time? I asked.

"No," he said curtly, barely acknowledging my presence.

He had obviously heard of my incredible tennis skills!

My most embarrassing moment on "Dune" came at a cocktail reception and dinner I organized. A group of international journalists had been flown into Mexico City to meet the filmmakers and cast. It was one of those open-my-mouth-and-put-my-foot-in-it—twice moments.

De Laurentiis, father and daughter and David Lynch were there as well as production designer Tony Masters and director of photography Freddie Francis. Among the actors who attended were Kyle MacLachlan and Francesca Annis, who played his mother, Lady Jessica.

Before we sat down to dinner I was chatting with Tony Masters and his wife, a former actress. I lifted my glass and offered a toast. "To you and yours," I said, indicating her swollen belly.

"I'm not pregnant, just fat," she said.

My face reddened and I mumbled an apology. I felt terrible, but I hadn't finished with her.

Once we were all at the long dinner table, I rose to introduce the various people connected with the film. I introduced Freddie Francis, the veteran British cinematographer "and sitting next to him, his lovely wife."

Except that she was Tony Masters' wife! She who was not pregnant.

Grinning, Freddie said, "We're very good friends, but that's as far as it goes. Honest!"

I'd managed to insult this poor woman in front of a group of people twice in just half an hour.

The next day Freddie Francis came over to me on the set and said, "You'd better watch out. I hear Tony Masters is looking for you."

On a much grander scale was an event that was several weeks in the

OF KINGS AND QUEENS AND MOVIE STARS

planning. We had invited about seventy theater owners from across the United States and Canada to spend three days in Mexico City.

Fred Skidmore and I spent some time in Mexico City together with Ronnie Chasen who was famed for her "fragile" state of health. On one occasion when we were visiting Mexico City's historical sites to plan a tour day for the visiting group, she suddenly declared that she did not feel well and disappeared for two days. We never did find out what was wrong with her, but continued our preparations, which included a visit to the pyramids outside the city.

Ronnie surpassed herself one evening when the three of us were dining at one of Mexico City's finest restaurants. She complained that her allergies were troubling her.

"I feel terrible. I'm going to be very sick. I know it. It's those plants. I'm very allergic to plants. Tell someone to take them away. They are making me very ill," she said, pointing to a planter behind our table.

"But they're plastic, my dear," Fred pointed out gently.

The visiting exhibitors were taken on a tour of the extraordinary sets. As they walked from desert scenery, through twisting tunnels, to palace throne rooms, stunt men would suddenly appear, locked in "mortal combat." Rocks collapsed and actors tumbled into the mouth of a giant sand worm. They witnessed the shooting of the climactic scene in the film when Kyle MacLachlan and Sting do battle. It was as if the Universal Studio tour or Disneyland had been brought into existence for just one day.

One stage had even been converted into a museum, with costumes, weapons, furniture, paraphernalia of all kinds, sketches and photographs on display. I got the biggest kick out of escorting Frank Herbert, author of the Dune books, on this tour. He was like a child in a candy shop, seeing the fruits of his imagination brought to existence for the first time.

"Yes, that's it, exactly what I had in mind," he would exclaim from time to time.

We treated our visitors to lunch alfresco on the studio grounds, giving everyone a special umbrella in case it rained—which it did. They were also given a souvenir bottle of tequila with a specially designed label declaring it a "Liquid Especial from the Desert Planet, Estate Bottled by the House of Atreides, A.D. 10983."

Old wines are valued, but I'm not sure about alcohol bottled nine thousand years in the future!

Shooting a motion picture of this scope in Mexico required certain delicate administrative decisions not normally needed when making a film north of the border. One full-time member of the staff was based at the Mexico City Airport. I don't remember his real name. We called him "Airport Harry". His sole function was to grease the palms of customs and immigration officials. "Harry" even carried a list of "fees," the amount of the bribe varying according to what and who was coming into the country.

Whenever I arrived, I was rushed through gates and doors by smiling officials, by-passing the usual long and tedious lines. My "fee" had been paid. Equipment or film stock arriving in Mexico, as it did on a daily basis, had a different, higher fee structure.

On one occasion I was asked to bring a camera lens with me from Los Angeles to replace a defective lens. It was a last minute request and I didn't tell our airport representative about it until I arrived. He was furious.

"What if the customs people had found it without my paying them off? It would have ruined everything," he said.

Of course, he was really angry because he had lost out on his percentage of the "fee." He knew better than anyone that nobody would be checking through my luggage. A few months after this incident this particular crew member was fired.

Corruption was rife in Mexico at this time. The best job you could get was that of a policeman. We had rented a coach to take our visiting exhibitors to see the pyramids outside Mexico City. The bus was stopped by a police officer who demanded to see our driver's license. He looked at it and said, "That is not your license. It is someone else's."

The driver apologized, slipped a banknote inside the license and returned it. The cop looked at it and said, "This photo looks more like you, but it's still not your license."

Once again the driver took his license back, slipped another note inside it and gave it back. This time the officer was satisfied. He got off the bus and waved us on with a smile.

Our production manager had had the foresight to hire the daughter of Mexico City's Chief of Police as a production assistant but, when she was

OF KINGS AND QUEENS AND MOVIE STARS

no longer needed, made the mistake of letting her go.

"You don't want to do that," she said.

"But I do. We really don't need you any more," he replied.

"Oh yes, you do," she insisted.

Despite her warnings, the girl was let go.

The next person to arrive in Mexico City from the States happened to be Greg Gorman, one of the world's top photographers, who had been hired to shoot portraits of our film's stars. He was arrested at the airport, his cameras and film confiscated. Greg languished in jail for three days until $10,000 was paid out by the production company and he was freed.

You really don't want to mess with the police chief's daughter!

My work on "Dune" was not limited to Mexico. With other Universal executives I made the trip to Atlanta, Georgia to make a presentation to the top brass at the Coca-Cola Company, which is headquartered in that city. We wanted to do a tie-in with them, centered on Coca-Cola glasses that would carry replicas of various "Dune" characters. We put together an impressive slide presentation, which showed the film's immense scope and exciting imagery.

After our show we were invited to have lunch in the executive dining room. White-gloved waiters offered us a variety of drinks including Coca-Cola, Diet Coke and their latest potion, Caffeine Free Coca-Cola. I opted for the newest addition to the soda stable. The senior executive vice-president sitting next to me waited nervously as I sipped at it as if it were a vintage wine.

"Well, what do you think?"

I let the liquid roll around my tongue, contemplated for a moment then pronounced my verdict.

"Delicious," I said.

The senior executive vice president beamed.

In truth, I rarely drink soda pop and can't tell the difference between Coke and Pepsi, let alone their hybrids.

The headquarters of Coca Cola is a strange place, like a cathedral devoted to bad drinking habits. Where most office buildings will have water coolers on each floor this place has soda dispensers and the stuff is free. People walk the corridors sipping at plastic cups as if they were taking the waters at a health spa. The staff regard their product with almost religious fervor.

Unfortunately they regarded "Dune" with less excitement and Universal was never able to do the deal.

It's a great shame that, with all the effort and money put into it, "Dune" didn't do well at the box office. People had said for years that the film could not be made. The story was too complex and obscure to make much sense in two hours of screen time. Those people were probably right.

***

While I was still working on the "Dune" project, Universal gave me the added responsibility of heading up the studio's international advertising and publicity department.

One of my first tasks in that capacity was to go back to Mexico for the filming of John Huston's "Under the Volcano", starring Albert Finney and Jacqueline Bissett. I arrived hours late in the city of Cuernavaca in the biggest downpour I had ever seen. My taxi driver appeared to be retarded, having no idea where my hotel was. We drove all over town, stopping now and then while I sloshed through foot deep water to ask directions. The driver stayed in his cab.

On reflection, perhaps the driver was taking me for a ride in more than one sense. Or maybe it was my Spanish.

This was the third Huston film I had been involved with, the others being "The Life and Times of Judge Roy Bean" for National General Pictures, and "Victory" for Lorimar. Huston had a reputation as a hell raiser when he was younger, but when I knew him he was always gracious.

Sadly, he was not a well man, suffering from the severe emphysema that would eventually kill him. He had an unusual method of directing caused, in part, by his physical handicap. He remained in a golf cart, equipped with oxygen tanks, staying some distance from the set he was directing, unable to see the actors directly. He watched the whole scene from a video monitor on his cart.

I had also worked on the international publicity for a number of other Jacqueline Bissett films— "Casino Royale", "The Grasshopper", "Who's Killing the Great Chefs of Europe" and the same "Life and Times of Judge Roy Bean." When she traveled to Paris to promote the latter film I organized

OF KINGS AND QUEENS AND MOVIE STARS

a birthday luncheon for her in the Halles district.

"Under the Volcano" is based on a classic story of alcoholism and betrayal, set in the 1920s. One morning on the set, while Jacqueline was wearing her period costume, I told her she reminded me of my mother from photos taken in that era. For some reason this angered her and she gave me a "how dare you!" glare and stormed off. I have no idea why she reacted this way. My mother had been an attractive young woman. In all fairness, I met Jacqueline again at a party I organized at the Beverly Hills Spago in 2001 and she could not have been more gracious. We've since become friends and I've invited her to numerous parties, notably a lunch with the director Paul Haggis, given to promote his film "Crash" in 2006. Happily it went on to win the 2005 Oscar for Best Picture.

***

JACK, THE EASY RIDER

In these days of computerized airline schedules…well, computerized everything, it's hard to imagine getting away with the deal that was swung for Jack Nicholson back in 1970.

We were preparing to leave Munich after promoting "Five Easy Pieces." Jack was a hot item following the runaway success of "Easy Rider." It was a morning flight to Paris and he had been kept up late the previous night.

I'm the sort of person who comes out in hives if I think I'm going to be at an airport less than an hour before departure time. Jack isn't.

So here I was, practically dragging him out of bed to catch the plane. Jack was in no hurry. Finally, I got him into the limo, convinced it was all a waste of time because there would be no plane waiting for us. I wasn't counting on our resourceful driver.

"No problem," he said, in the manner of such people the world over.

He had a car phone, rare in the prehistoric days before cellular phones. It was simply a matter of calling the airline and asking them to hold the flight. Mr. Nicholson was running a little late, he explained.

"No problem," said the airline.

Sure enough, arriving 20 minutes after departure time, we were politely boarded and were soon on our way to Paris. I didn't ask any of the other passengers what they thought about the delay.

While on the subject of "Easy Rider," I have a confession to make.

Hollywood studios screen films for their sales and marketing executives both in the United States and abroad, in order to gain their input. European and French executives screened "Easy Rider" at the company offices on the rue Troyon in Paris.

When the showing ended we all looked at each other. Here was a very different film about hippies and motorcycles. The dialogue was strange, the open smoking of marijuana was unheard of and we were all quite convinced the film would be a disaster outside the United States.

I found the film interesting, but totally uncommercial. I was wrong.

OF KINGS AND QUEENS AND MOVIE STARS

The low budget film ($400,000) has become a very successful classic. Its $7 million gross may be peanuts today but a quarter of a century ago that was not small change. A seventeen-fold return on your investment isn't bad in any decade. I mention this because I am probably the only person working for Columbia Pictures at that time who would admit that he thought "Easy Rider" would bomb.

To paraphrase someone else's clever remark—success has a hundred fathers, failure is an orphan.

***

FABULOUS FULLER

Director Sam Fuller was one of the great Hollywood characters. Though short in stature he was larger than life.

He is regarded as the father of films noir, with such films of the late fifties and early sixties as "Pick Up On South Street," "Shock Corridor," "The Naked Kiss" and "Dead Pigeon on Beethoven Street." Sam was a crime reporter for various newspapers, author of several books and a producer and screenwriter. During the Second World War he served in the 1st Infantry Division of the United States Army—The Big Red One.

He wrote a book about his wartime experiences, but it took him 35 years to put it on the screen. The film was produced by Gene Corman for Lorimar in 1980, when I was head of international advertising and publicity for the company.

I spent a lot of time with him promoting the film and we became good friends. With his rasping, staccato speech shooting out like machine gun bullets round the Monte Cristo cigar permanently wedged between his teeth, Sam could be a little intimidating to those who first met him.

His first words to someone could well be an insult coming from anyone else, but when Sam said "You're a scrawny piece of nothing!" as a form of greeting, he was just kidding.

Barely known in the U.S., Sam Fuller is considered an icon of the American cinema by the French. When we were at the Cannes Film Festival he would sit in a chair by his hotel pool with acolytes at his knees all day long. They would listen or take notes and Sam would talk. And boy, could Sam talk. He rattled off one anecdote after another and usually was at it until two or three in the morning. Though in his sixties at the time, he had more energy than the twenty or thirty something cinephiles who listened to his every word.

We made a trip to Madrid one time to give the film a boost in Spain. Sarita Montiel, darling of the Spanish screen and stage, had starred in one of his films many years earlier. We heard that she was doing a one woman musical show in town, so Sam determined to look her up.

As we entered the large auditorium Sarita stopped in mid-song and yelled from the stage, "My God, it's Sam Fuller."

We made our way to our seats, Sarita arriving there soon after us. She climbed on to Sam's lap, gave him a loud kiss then returned to the stage, explaining to the audience her relationship with the "great American director."

Sam Fuller directed one American film after "The Big Red One"—"White Dog." The picture was beset with distribution and censorship problems.

Sadly, he left his house on Woodrow Wilson Drive in the Hollywood Hills (he called it his shack) and moved to France with his wife Christa and daughter Samantha, to be where his genius could be recognized. I had dinner at his Paris home in 1986 and was glad to see that he was still working, both as a director and writer.

He gave me a copy of his book La Grande Mêlée ("Battle Royal") with the inscription, "To Leonard: Who has the honor to like a pleasant melee now and then."

Sam had seen me in some of my more impatient modes. Anything can bring them on. Most of the time I'm friendly, easy going, then someone will come along who is rude or pushy. Explosion! In particular he may have remembered my garden party fight with a photographer at the Cannes Film Festival.

Sam did return to live in his Los Angeles "shack" before he died.

***

SWEDEN AND OTHER PLACES

Today we think of Sweden as the epitome of a modern state, very much in tune to the latest fashions in music and film. It wasn't that way in 1963 when I was there with Ann-Margret.

She was born in Sweden and, with her parents, had moved to America at the age of 12. Now, ten years later, she and her parents were back home for the first time—to promote the musical "Bye Bye Birdie" in which she starred with Janet Leigh and Dick Van Dyke.

With all the fuss that was made, you'd think she was in Stockholm to receive the Nobel Prize. I'd never seen such press coverage. Every daily newspaper carried front page stories each day of her stay there. Television, radio and magazines were clamoring for interviews or photo sessions. Wherever we went huge crowds were waiting and I had to force a way through the throng. I wish all publicity junkets were that productive.

Ann-Margret was the first Swedish actress to make it in Hollywood since Greta Garbo and Ingrid Bergman, and everybody wanted a piece of her. Her aunts and uncles traveled down from their homes in the north of the country for a touching family reunion.

On the night of the premiere we held a party at one of Stockholm's grand hotels. The Swedes were a stodgy lot in those days and were still dancing the fox-trot, quick step and waltz. The Beatles and all the changes they were to foster had not yet melted the frozen north. To be honest, at that time, I wasn't too much aware of the Beatles and their brand of music myself. Ann-Margret straightened that out. She showed me all the latest steps to the bemusement of all who watched.

Fortunately I was able to repay her for her instructions by acting as a discreet cupid. She had just fallen in love with actor Roger Smith but didn't want her parents to know about it. So she used me to send him love telegrams and to intercept his replies. Of course, they married later and are still happily married.

***

OF KINGS AND QUEENS AND MOVIE STARS

Let's get back to that tour to promote Carl Foreman's "The Victors". We had left our intrepid group at the royal premiere in Stockholm ("A ROYAL PAIN"). The following afternoon we took the hour's flight to Copenhagen to attend the Danish opening of the film. Carl had to go straight on to London where he had urgent business. A limo was waiting for George Hamilton, Senta Berger and myself. We chatted in the airport V.I.P. lounge with Columbia's Danish publicity manager while waiting for our bags to arrive. We chatted, we waited, we chatted some more. I decided to do some checking and found our luggage—on its way to Paris!

Here I was with two stars about to appear at a glamorous premiere and we didn't have so much as a toothbrush between us. George and Senta took it all in their stride. Another actress might have demanded that we rush out and buy her an evening gown, but Senta just grinned and said it was no big deal. She appeared at the premiere in the heavy boots and topcoat she had been wearing on the plane. Our luggage arrived the following morning, so they were able to change their clothes for the media interviews that had been set up by our local office.

George Hamilton is a gregarious man who likes to enjoy himself. Until now, he and I had been out on the town every night. On our last evening in Copenhagen he begged off, explaining that he was tired. He didn't look tired but I was happy to have an evening to myself. On the plane the following day he said to me, "You're probably wondering why I didn't want to go out last night."

I told him that I had thought it out of character.

"Didn't you get a look at my chambermaid?" he asked. "That's what kept me in my room."

***

The next stop on our tour was Berlin. Here we were joined by their co-star, Romy Schneider, another Austrian actress, who was a big star in France, where she lived.

That evening we were all driven to the Zoo Palast cinema for the premiere. The film had barely started when Romy stood up and rushed out of the theater. Worried, I hurried after her and caught up with her in the street. She did not want to talk but allowed me to escort her back to the

Hotel Kempinski.

We sat down in the hotel lobby where she suddenly burst into tears. She buried her head in my shoulders. Not quite sure how to handle this problem I tentatively patted her back and asked her what was wrong.

Between sobs, she told me that she had just been dumped by Alain Delon, France's reigning movie king, with whom she had been having a highly public affair. I held her in my arms for a long time until her tears had subsided. We returned to the cinema before the end of the movie. No one realized the trauma she had just gone through as she joined her co-stars to accept the audience applause.

Romy was so beautiful and vivacious it was easy to get her on the cover of just about any magazine. Yet, in spite of her success she was a very unhappy woman. Several years later she suffered the tragic death of her small son. The boy had tried to climb the wrought iron fence surrounding their Paris home, probably because it was more fun than walking through the gate. He had slipped and impaled himself on an iron spike. He died a slow and agonizing death. Romy couldn't take it. She became a recluse and later took her life.

***

ON TARGET

In the fall of 1984 I moved back to Paris, ten years after I had left that city to live in California. It was wonderful to be back, even if would be for only four months this time. Of the half dozen countries and various cities I've lived in, Paris is the only place I miss when I'm not there.

I arrived at my hotel at nine in the morning, flying directly from Los Angeles. Of course my room wasn't ready yet so I took a walk along the familiar streets. I found myself near the offices of Columbia Pictures where I had stopped working some 13 years earlier. Suddenly breakfast at the tabac across the street seemed very attractive. The same one-eyed waiter I had known those many years ago was polishing the bar. He barely looked up when I ordered my café and tartine beurré.

"Bonjour, M'sieur," he said casually.

"You don't remember me, do you?" I asked.

"Of course I do," he replied, with all the conviction of a kid denying he'd been at the cookie jar.

Yeah, right, I thought.

He walked to the other end of the bar to take care of another customer.

In a couple of minutes he was back.

"Tell me, M'sieur Morpurgo, how are your wife and two sons these days?"

My mouth dropped open. I wasn't aware that he had ever known my name, let alone that he would remember it or my family.

This is what I like about Parisians. There's no bullshit, no "have a nice day." What you see is what you get. Many Americans don't like the French because they are used to the insincere friendliness we often find here in California.

I returned to my hotel, opened my suitcase, grabbed a tennis racket and tennis clothes and took a taxi out to the suburb of Meudon where I had lived for many years. I was anxious to see my friends at the Standard Athletic Club, a unique British sports club, hidden deep in the Forest of

Meudon. When I lived here before, I spent every weekend at the club, playing tennis when the weather permitted and bridge when it didn't. So far as I know this is the only place in France where you can see a cricket match every weekend during the summer. Local residents, out for a stroll, would peer through the hedges at this strange sport anglais.

Returning to the club after all these years was like entering a time warp. The same people were sitting in the same seats in the clubhouse dishing the same gossip. A few more lines, a little more gray hair, some new faces, but not much had changed. They were delighted to see me. I was home.

I could fill another book with stories from the Standard Athletic Club, but I'll relate just one of my favorites here. An English couple, members of the club, decided to get an amicable divorce. As there was no "no fault" divorce in France at the time one of them had to be guilty of something. The man, whom I will call "Fred," felt that as an English gentleman he should shoulder that responsibility. They decided on adultery, but he didn't know anyone who would do the deed with him. Eventually they came to an arrangement and Fred was duly surprised in a hotel room by a detective hired for the purpose. The woman who was lying in bed with Fred refused to give her name to the detective, but her being there was sufficient cause and the divorce went through. This mysterious adulteress was, in fact, Fred's wife, committing "adultery" with her own husband.

I rejoined the club on a temporary basis during my four months stay and it was as if I had never been away. After a few days I left my hotel and moved into a magnificent apartment in Neuilly, next to the Bois de Boulogne and looking out over the Seine.

The reason for this 1984 trip was the filming of "Target", produced by Richard Zanuck and David Brown for CBS Theatrical Films and distributed in the United States by Warner Bros. Filming was to take place in Hamburg and Texas as well as Paris, with Arthur Penn as director.

This was the first time I had done unit publicity. Until now I had merely supervised unit publicists, so I suppose my career was growing in reverse.

A word of explanation may be in order here. A unit publicist is a member of the film crew. On larger scale movies such as "Target" it's a full-time, on the set every day, position. His job is to bring media on to the set and arrange interviews with the stars, director or producer; to write a press

OF KINGS AND QUEENS AND MOVIE STARS 85

kit, which is an information package used by press, distributors and other interested parties; and to supervise the unit still photographer. The still photographer takes those photos you see in theater lobbies, newspapers and magazines or part of an advertisement.

The unit publicist will also work closely with the makers of the electronic press kit, a video package using interviews of the principals, and background filming, for television programs such as Entertainment Tonight. He handles V.I.P. visits to the set and generally gets in everyone's way.

As he contributes absolutely nothing to the making of the movie, he is sometimes thought of as a necessary evil by those actually creating this masterpiece (or piece of garbage, depending on the film).

I arrived on the set at the Boulogne Studios in the southwest suburbs of Paris and presented myself to David Brown, the avuncular husband of Cosmopolitan's then editor, Helen Gurley Brown. He invited me to lunch. As we were eating, Arthur Penn entered. David got up to introduce me when Arthur shouted across the room, "My God, it's Leonard isn't it? Didn't we meet in Venice in 1965?" We had indeed met briefly in Venice when I was promoting his film "Mickey One" at the Festival there. There was little likelihood that he'd have remembered me. In truth, he hadn't remembered me. He was just setting me up.

The two stars of "Target" were Gene Hackman and Matt Dillon, then 20 years old. Gene was professional and easy-going, though occasionally moody. Matt was difficult. On the last day of filming, at Dallas Fort Worth Airport in Texas, Gene made a point of coming up and apologizing for his sometimes sullen attitude to me. It had been a tough shoot, he explained. I told him an apology certainly wasn't necessary. I was aware that the times when he seemed to disappear inside himself were his way of concentrating.

A short while later Matt came over and said, "You are one lucky man. There were many times on this shoot when I wanted to kill you, but you were never around."

"That's why I'm a good publicist. I know when to disappear," I responded.

I had been told when I arrived on the film that Hackman didn't like to do interviews unless they were major pieces. Fair enough. Dillon really didn't like to do interviews at all, particularly television interviews.

Nevertheless, I did persuade him to do a few TV shots and I understood why he didn't like them. He was inarticulate in front of the camera and knew it.

He became particularly angry over a newspaper article for which he hadn't even been interviewed. Mary Blume, a veteran writer for the International Herald Tribune, whom I had known for 20 years, came to the studio to interview Arthur Penn. She understood that a director doesn't have too much time to give interviews while working, so she was content to sit and watch until there was a lighting or scene change. Arthur, who was always gracious, would come over and talk to her for ten or fifteen minutes, then return to filming when he was called. This interview by installments took two or three hours.

In her article, Mary wrote of the scene she was watching that Gene Hackman came on to the set, always knew his lines and was thoroughly professional. Dillon, on the other hand, stumbled over his words repeatedly and held everyone up while his scenes were re-shot.

Someone made the mistake of showing Matt the article when it appeared the following week. This happened to be a bad day anyway. We were filming in a cold, damp airline hanger near the town of Mantes-la-Jolie, with the weather miserable and drizzly. Everything was going wrong. Even Penn was in a bad mood. Dillon was furious. He stormed over to where I was standing in a corner of the hanger, waving the "Trib" under my nose. "How dare you have a reporter on the set without getting my approval," he yelled.

I pointed out that Mary had not been there to interview him and had not even spoken to him. She had only written what she had observed while waiting for Arthur Penn.

"But she saw me working in a very stressful and difficult scene. In future, no press come on to the set without my OK."

He was so agitated that I think he would have hit me if a second assistant director hadn't arrived to tell him he was wanted for the next scene. I wisely failed to point out that all his scenes were stressful and difficult.

In fairness to Dillon, my experience with him was not all negative. We went out together in the evenings from time to time and I had a glimpse of how difficult life can be for a young star. He couldn't go out in public

OF KINGS AND QUEENS AND MOVIE STARS

without being besieged by young fans, and beneath all his bluster he was just a shy kid, alone in a strange city where people spoke a strange language. Most evenings he spent alone, reading.

[I got to meet a very different Matt Dillion in 2006 when promoting the film "Crash." It went on to win the Best Film Academy Award and Matt received glowing reviews for his performance. He was self-assured, friendly and bore no grudges.]

While filming "Target" Hackman and Dillon, who played father and son, didn't get on well. Matt told Gene that he had never taken an acting class in his life and thought it was a waste of time. Gene considered him unprofessional. During one scene Hackman got so mad that he almost reduced the younger actor to tears. Hackman was on camera speaking to an off camera Dillon. Matt, who knew that the lines he spoke on this camera angle would not be used in the film, just mumbled his words, never looking at Hackman who therefore had nothing to play off.

Their mutual dislike was so extreme that I couldn't get them to pose together for our photographer until almost the last day of shooting, when we were back in the United States.

"Do I have to pretend to like him?" Gene asked me, after they had both finally agreed to do the shot.

"You can handle it. You're a good actor," I said.

Gene Hackman is also a dedicated actor. A scene to be shot in the Hamburg harbor called for him to jump into the water to escape a fusillade of bullets. A stunt man was available and Arthur Penn was quite happy to use him, but Gene, a strong swimmer and former U.S. Navy diver, insisted on shooting the scene himself even though he was suffering from a strained knee.

"I want the audience to see clearly that it's me in the water," he told me. The Elbe River in Hamburg is the most treacherous stretch of water in Europe. The current is so powerful that authorities would allow us to shoot the scene only during a 35-minute period when the tide is changing and at its most docile.

To add to the dangers, the water is highly polluted and Hamburg was going through one of its most severe winters.

Gene, wearing a wet suit under his clothing, made the leap without a complaint. Police frogmen waited off camera in case he got into trouble. A stunt man was used for other camera angles where Gene's face would not be seen.

Hackman is a down-to-earth guy, not the sort you would expect to have psychic prescience, yet one day during filming at the Paris studio he showed that ability.

Let me set the scene. In the plot, an assassin had been stalking the Hackman character. The bad guy, played by Jean-Pol Dubois, follows Hackman up to his hotel room, but is himself shot to death by Hackman. He was supposed to slide down to the floor, leaving a bullet hole and a smear of blood on the mirrored door behind him.

Jean-Pol, who had become a good friend of mine in the weeks we had been working together, was in a black mood before the shooting. He sat in a corner by himself and wouldn't talk to me. The scene was carefully rehearsed. Jean-Pol was fitted with a "blood" pack under his shirt. The mirror was rigged with an electric charge. When the pistol was fired, both the pack and the mirror were set off by a technician hiding behind the door.

Although the scene called for Hackman to fire the gun, his presence was not really necessary for this angle, so he was sitting in the studio bar while this was going on.

I stood next to Arthur Penn, who fired the gun himself. Blood spurted from the pack on Jean-Pol's chest. He slid to the floor revealing the blood and shattered mirror, but instead of just lying there he started twitching uncontrollably.

Boy, I thought, he sure is milking this scene. He didn't do this during rehearsal. The crew waited for him to stop emoting. Then Penn realized that blood was not only coming from the chest, but was also running down his face and the side of his neck. That was not supposed to happen.

Arthur rushed to the ashen-faced and still twitching Jean-Pol. Blood was now pouring from his neck. We soon figured out what had happened. A transparent coating on the mirror, which was supposed to prevent it from shattering, had dried out under the studio lights and instead of a neat round hole appearing in the glass, hundreds of tiny shards had blown out like minute missiles. Jean-Pol had just turned his neck and received the full force of the explosion. Several pieces of glass had missed the carotid artery by millimeters.

An ambulance was called and Jean-Pol was taken to the hospital, where doctors spent several hours removing the glass from his neck and face.

I looked up Gene in the bar and told him what had happened. He did not even seem surprised.

"I knew it was going to happen. I dreamed last night that Jean-Pol was going to be injured," he said.

Jean-Pol had also had a premonition, which accounted for his own somber mood.

We had to wait a month to re-shoot the scene to give Jean-Pol time to heal. This time the special effects crew used a manual technique. They simply punched a hole in the mirror with a metal rod as the gun was fired. Jean-Pol was his usual relaxed self and the scene went through without any problems or undue twitching.

The Russian actress, Victoria Fyodorova played a former CIA agent in "Target", which was a deep irony. The Russian secret police, the KGB, had played a major role in her own life and had almost destroyed it. One evening she told me her story, a story that brought anger to her voice and tears to her large green luminous eyes as she recalled those dramatic events, set on a canvas as broad as the Russian steppes.

Before and during the Second World War, Victoria's mother, Zoya, had been the Soviet Union's leading movie star. The nation's second most powerful—and dangerous man after Stalin was the evil Lavrenty Beria, head of the KGB. Towards the end of the war he told Zoya that he wanted to sleep with her. She told him to take a look in the mirror. She didn't sleep with monkeys, she said. That was not something you told Beria, but he simply bowed and told an assistant to escort her to her car. A bouquet of roses lay on the back seat. Zoya told the aide that Beria was presumptuous in giving her flowers. The aide said Zoya didn't understand. They were for her grave.

A few months later Zoya attended a cocktail party in honor of foreign minister Molotov. Across a crowded room she saw the man who would change her life, an American naval captain, Jackson Tate. Her heart exploded—a Molotov cocktail, if you will. They consummated their love on Victory Day. Nine months later Victoria was born, named for the day on which she had been conceived.

After a further nine months, the patient Beria began to spin his evil web. The American captain was declared persona non grata and Zoya was sent out of town so that he could not contact her before leaving the country. She was arrested and thrown into prison, her crime, sleeping with the enemy. Baby Victoria and her aunt were sent into exile in Siberia, where the child was named an Enemy of the People. She grew up, believing her aunt was her mother and not understanding why she was taunted by the other children and given meatless rations.

Times changed. Stalin died and was replaced by Malenkov. In 1953 Beria was tried and executed. Khrushchev assumed power later that year and began freeing the hundreds of thousands of political prisoners, including Victoria, now nine years old. She was sent on the long train journey to Moscow to live with an "aunt" she didn't know existed. After several months the "aunt" revealed that she was in fact her real mother. Five years later she told Victoria who her father was.

The girl began a 15-year quest to find him. She had meanwhile followed in her mother's footsteps and had become an actress, first on the stage, then as a star of numerous Russian films. Eventually, in 1975, she was given a 90-day visa and allowed to travel to the United States to meet her father. She had traced him to Florida where he had retired with the rank of admiral.

At their tearful meeting he explained that he had tried to find her mother for years but she had written that she was happily married, had other children and never wanted to hear from him again. The letters were KGB forgeries.

Then history was repeated. At a cocktail party at her father's home, given in her honor, Victoria met and immediately fell in love with Frederick Pouy, a Pan Am pilot. With her visa about to run out, they were married two weeks later.

In 1980 Victoria wrote a book about her dramatic life. It was called "The Admiral's Daughter" and became a best seller. Plans were made to make a movie of it starring Sophia Loren. A year after publication of the book someone entered Zoya Fyodorova's home in an elegant section of

OF KINGS AND QUEENS AND MOVIE STARS

Moscow and shot her dead. Although money and jewelry were in plain sight nothing was stolen. Neighbors heard nothing and police who patrolled the area saw nothing. The official investigation was brief and inconclusive. No newspaper carried a story about the killing or even an obituary, even though she was one of the country's best-loved stars. It was obviously the work of the KGB.

"But Beria had been dead for years," I said.

"Yes," Victoria replied bitterly, "but his friends have long memories."

Neither of us mentioned that the publication of her book had possibly awakened memories among Beria's old friends.

The movie of "The Admiral's Daughter" was never made.

This is, of course, a tragic story, but tragedies don't always occur through murder, imprisonment or betrayal. Sometimes tragedies can be like dripping taps, destroying through erosion, slowly, inevitably.

One such tragedy belonged to Herbert Berghof, who was 75 at this time. In "Target" he portrayed Hackman's long-time East German nemesis. Berghof, with his wife, Uta Hagen, has taught thousands of today's screen and stage actors. His New York acting studio was one of the most respected in the United States.

He started his prestigious acting and directing career in his native Vienna back in 1927, where he was a member of the Max Reinhardt Seminar. He came to the United States in 1939 where he became a charter member of the Actors Studio, forming his own acting studio in 1954. For five decades he has been one of the nation's most celebrated and sought after actors.

In other words, this man had credentials.

Off the set, he was a delight to talk to, funny and warm and full of wonderful stories. On the set, he couldn't remember his lines. His advancing years had worn away his short-term memory. He couldn't remember more than three or four words at a time in front of the camera. It was as painful for us to watch him as it must have been for him to go through this agony. Again and again he would stumble, apologize and start over. Arthur Penn was patient and understanding. Hours were spent on Berghof's scenes, shot in tiny slivers from every conceivable angle.

Watching the dailies (unedited scenes shot the previous day) one evening, I asked Penn how he could possibly use any of the Berghof material.

"Don't worry! Once the editors have finished with this, we'll have an Oscar winning performance out of Herbert," he told me.

Sure enough, all those bits and pieces were threaded together through the magic of the editing room. If you get the opportunity to rent a DVD of "Target" you will see that, indeed, Herbert Berghof gives a masterful performance.

***

CANNES CAN DO

I've already told a few stories about the Cannes Film Festival. This chapter tells a whole lot more about this most glamorous event in the film industry's calendar.

Although I began going to film festivals in 1963, I didn't attend Cannes until 1973, when I was working independently out of Paris. I started doing this festival on a regular basis in 1979, after I'd joined Lorimar.

Cannes is a bewildering place for first timers. Activities are spread out throughout the mile long Croisette. On the east side of town is the Martinez Hotel; the Carlton Hotel, with its famous terrace, is in the middle next to it the Noga Hilton, newly renamed the Hotel Palais Stephanie and on the western side can be found the Majestic Hotel, across from the Palais des Festivals, where the official screenings are held.

In conjunction with the festival there's a market, which means exactly what it says. Producers and distributors set up offices in the four hotels mentioned, on yachts and in apartments. In recent years the Riviera complex, adjacent to the Palais has become an expo all by itself. Dozens of sales companies take booths in this huge complex, which takes away some of the glamour that is Cannes. Close by is the International Village, featuring rows of pavilions representing many nations. The American Pavilion has become an important meeting place for ex-patriot Yanks. Buyers from around the world make the exhausting trip round the hotels, to the harbor, to the Riviera building, searching for the films they need, bartering, schmoozing and complaining how expensive everything is. This is a time-honored tradition. Not once have I heard a buyer say that film quality is high and prices are fair.

If the official black tie screenings can be thought of as Broadway, these market movies are off off Broadway. They are shown in private screenings in the city's theaters, mostly on the chic rue d'Antibes, and in screening rooms in the Riviera.

Producers who attend screenings of their prized movies for the first time here are horrified. Rarely does anyone stay to see an entire picture. They'll check out a film for 10 minutes, then move on to the screening in the next room. Producers are not used to that, but these international buyers simply don't have the time.

Some professionals come here to work, others to party. And there are plenty of parties during the Festival's twelve days in May. On any given evening half a dozen cocktail parties are going strong at one of the beach restaurants that run the length of the Croisette, in one of the elegant hotels or on board a yacht rented for the duration. Then there are dinners given by distributors for their clients and, later, huge parties for up to 2,000 people at a nightclub taken over for the occasion or at one of the two casinos.

Of course, while all this is going on the official Festival is grinding out two black tie screenings a night. Here you will see your international stars climbing the broad, elegant staircase lined by smartly dressed guards. Hundreds of photographers and television cameras jostle for space and crowds patiently wait to see their favorite star, or maybe just a familiar face.

Media coverage is enormous. More than 3,000 press are officially registered every year and it can be a nightmare for a publicist to reach the journalist or camera crew he wants. The festival authorities do issue lists of accredited press and where they are staying, but it's usually not available until four days into the festival; which leaves you on your own until then. Even then it can be tough. You can leave a message at a hotel or pass the word round that you have a photo call or press conference. Notices can be posted at certain strategic spots and each journalist has a mail box at the palais—which he never looks in.

When I returned to Cannes in 2006, after an eight-year hiatus, I found that modern technology had made things simpler. If you do your homework and learn the cell phone numbers of key press before you leave your home base then they are obviously easier to reach. Before the common use of email I had to walk and walk. One year I calculated that I had walked a hundred miles, up and down the Croisette, in and out of hotels.

Five trade publications appear every day and much of my time revolves around their deadlines and setting up interviews or delivering stories to their reporters. Added stress will come from ego-swollen producers, stars

OF KINGS AND QUEENS AND MOVIE STARS

or directors.

One of the daily hassles is to obtain tickets to a hot screening for clients or for visiting V.I.P.s. The cliché says that hell hath no fury like a woman scorned. That ain't nothin'. Try facing the ire of someone who thinks he is important and whom you have not been able to get into a screening or a party.

In some ways I dread this circus, but I also look forward to it. This is an opportunity to meet old friends from around the world and to make new ones. When I don't have to organize an evening event myself, I enjoy going out to one of the excellent restaurants in and around the town with a group of buddies. I rarely see one of the official movies, maybe one each year. It hardly seems worth the effort and when I get tickets I usually end up giving them to friends, anxious to get in.

***

About five years after I'd organized the "Being There" party already mentioned, I was having a quiet drink on the Carlton Hotel terrace. I heard my name being bellowed out by a familiar voice. Robin Leach, he of the "Lifestyles of the Rich and Famous", was trying to attract my attention.

"I remember when you gave that party at the Eden Roc for Peter Sellers," he said. "You had to pay $200,000 in cash and when you didn't have it they made you stay there overnight until you could get the money."

"It was $50,000 and I did have enough and they were very happy to get it," I replied.

"Well, that's not the way I tell the story," he said, closing the conversation.

***

My first year working for CBS Theatrical Films I planned a party for about 80 distributors in a small restaurant on a hillside in le Suquet, Cannes' old town. We had taken over a large room at the rear of the restaurant and I had painstakingly put place names at every seat. As the room began to fill, the producer Freddie Fields appeared, accompanied by soccer super star, Pele. He had heard about the dinner and had decided to crash it. I had no idea what to do.

"Sure I have a table. Follow me," I told him. I led them through the restaurant and out the door. We were standing in the middle of the narrow street.

"I'll have a table set up for you here, because that's the only place there's room."

He looked at me aghast and I relented. After all, Freddie was an important Hollywood figure and Pele was a super hero. I spoke to the restaurant owner and was able to get them a table in the small outer room and charged it to our party.

***

One of the most villainous characters in movie history, right along with Dracula and Frankenstein's monster, is the steel-toothed "Jaws" of the James Bond films. He is portrayed by Richard Kiel, a sweet giant and devoted father. Richard was in Cannes with his wife and young son to promote his children's film "The Giant of Thunder Mountain" in which he portrays a misunderstood and outcast mountain man.

Richard's is a sad story. He suffers from gigantism, a disease in which the pituitary growth gland runs wild. A huge man, a giant in the literal sense, his organs are still growing and he knows that the disease will eventually kill him. In Cannes he was in constant pain and could hardly walk. It was a major effort for him to make it from my office to a car parked 20 yards away.

Yet, unlike many of the people I've had to deal with in Cannes, he never complained. We went to a special Saturday morning screening I had set up for a group of local children and he happily posed for them. When the house lights came on after the screening they were a little scared to find this man, who could make James Bond look like a wimp, standing in the theater, but he soon put them at ease. He became a pied piper with children following him wherever he went.

***

The Cannes Film Festival is right up there with Congress and other gatherings of politicians in producing voluminous amounts of hot air. Certain companies are famous for trumpeting forthcoming productions that everyone in the industry knows will never be made. I'm not sure how much of it is wishful thinking and how much a deliberate scam. Probably somewhere in between. They figure that if they can get enough international buyers to advance money for rights to a film then they can afford to make it. Some producers would announce 40 or 50 such films each year in the daily Cannes trade papers, on expensive billboards in hotels and on the street, through stunts and via press conferences. This used to work, but in recent years buyers have become cagey, having been burned a few times too many.

It's also been harder for these infamous companies, who are very, very slow payers, to get their advertisements and billboards accepted by trades and hotels. Each year a few of them fall by the wayside, but other companies, run by the same executives, replace them, only to disappear in turn a few years later.

To outsiders, the Cannes Film Festival is a playground for the rich and glamorous. Yes, they are there, but most professionals who attend spend much of their time worrying how they're going to pay their hotel bills.

I've had my share of perpetrating ballyhoo on the already cynical media, but usually it was with good intent.

A few years ago, when I was with the Michael Dalling P.R. Company, we represented a client who had closed a deal with the John Mills family to produce a film in which they would all be starring. For the first time in his long and illustrious career Sir John Mills attended the Cannes Film Festival, along with his wife, Mary Hayley Bell, daughter Hayley Mills and Hayley's son, Crispin, to announce the film, titled "The Last Straw." With much trumpeting we announced that they, plus daughter Juliet Mills, would all be acting in the same film for the first time. To make it even more of a family affair, the screenplay had been written by Sir John's son, Jonathan. It was the delightful story of a man (Sir John) brought home from an old people's home. The only family member who could get on with him was his grandson played by real-life grandson, Crispin.

We held a press conference at the Carlton, followed by a lunch on the beach with British journalist, David Lewin. From there a limousine whisked them to Nice Airport whence they returned home to England.

It was a good story and there was a lot of coverage, particularly in the British press. The only problem was that the film was never made. A couple of months after Cannes one of the financial partners dropped out and with that the project died.

***

A different kind of ballyhoo surrounded a Russian entrepreneur by the name of Ismael Tagi-Zade. Shortly before the break-up of the Soviet Union he headed the Association of Soviet Film and Television Distributors (ASKIN), a semi-private group that had the virtual monopoly on theaters throughout the USSR.

Tagi-Zade is a charismatic individual who started his career by selling flowers in the Moscow subway, hiring railroad employees to moonlight for him. They made more money with flowers than with trains. With his profits he bought a few Arabian horses, bred them and built up a business with the West. He had a couple of clothing factories and his movie business. His theaters showed movies from the West exclusively, to the considerable annoyance of the entrenched icons of the Soviet film industry.

During the Brezhnev era the Communists rejected all his attempts to join the Party, his business dealings being considered too odious. Towards the end of Gorbachev's regime he was finally admitted, just when everyone else was leaving.

Tagi-Zade speaks no English, but through an interpreter he told me that he considered himself half capitalist, half Communist.

"One grandfather owned oil fields, my other grandfather was a Bolshevik who was killed during the revolution."

I first met Ismael in Los Angeles. Michael Dalling and I had been asked to organize a party on his behalf during the American Film Market. He was bringing 60 ASKIN members to L.A. for the occasion. I selected the newly built Armand Hammer Museum in Westwood as the location because of Hammer's Russian interests.

The party, for about 400 people, was a huge success. Tagi-Zade and his group had brought cases of vodka and five kilos of caviar with them and that would make any party go well.

OF KINGS AND QUEENS AND MOVIE STARS

This, however, was nothing compared with the party we were asked to organize in Cannes two or three months later to promote his film "Ivan the Terrible." We booked the huge banqueting room in the Palais des Festivals and 1,500 people showed up. This was a good turn-out considering that Madonna was hosting a party for 2,000 the other side of town. She got the celebrity seekers. We got the eaters and drinkers.

I arrived at the party 40 minutes ahead of time to find more than 200 people already waiting for the doors to open. They had heard about our caviar and vodka. Most of those waiting were local people who had nothing to do with the industry. Somehow they had all managed to get invitations. This time Ismail had brought 11 kilos of caviar and I even managed to eat some of it myself before being trampled by voracious hordes.

Earlier in the day he had brought Cannes to a standstill by having a parade of Russian actors, singers, dancers and horses march down the Croisette on their way to perform outside city hall.

He brought 120 ASKIN members with him so that they could see "how wonderful everything is in the West and strive to make a life like that for themselves." Unfortunately, his members had even less money than everyone else, so all they could do was wander the streets and gape at all the wealth and glamour that surrounded them.

The strongest vision locked in my memory comes from the end of our big party. Most of the guests had already moved on to other social gatherings. Only the Soviets were left, standing in small circles singing their melancholy songs, swaying slightly, their voices blurred. It was a sad moment. The opulent West was already just a dream and they hadn't yet left.

Ismael Tagi-Zade made the mistake of boasting that the whole venture cost $1 million. This didn't go down too well with the folks back home who were struggling to survive. I attended a press conference he gave for the Soviet media. I didn't understand anything being said, but it was obvious he was being pilloried.

Two days before the festival ended, when most festival goers had already gone home, he asked us to invite people to a small party he was giving that evening, poolside on the roof of the Savoy Hotel. He asked me what we would charge to do that. Jokingly I told him it would cost him a case of vodka. He didn't know I was joking and that is exactly how we were paid.

A few months later the Soviet Union and its Communist Party disappeared on to the scrap heap of history. Tagi-Zade, victim of his own extravagance, boasting and bad timing, disappeared too.

***

The stresses of Cannes can bring out the worst in people. Shapiro/Glickenhaus, a now defunct American production and distribution company, had hired the Michael Dalling Company to get the media to a huge party they were giving at the Studio Circus nightclub to honor their film "Red Dawn." Dolf Lundgren, the star, would attend and they would screen 40 minutes of the film at the party. I didn't think the screening was a very good idea and I turned out to be right. People don't go to nightclubs to see movies, they go to see and be seen.

I arrived early to save a group of seats for some key journalists we had invited, including the editor of Variety. They were clearly marked 'reserved'. Nevertheless, a young woman decided she wanted to be there and clambered over backs of chairs to make it. I touched her shoulder and told her the seats were taken. She ignored me and sat down anyway. Her companion, a particularly unpleasant American producer, started yelling at me, screaming epithets and warning that he'd beat the crap out of me if I laid my hands on his friend again. When I tried to explain the situation he became even more volatile.

He was an important producer and I was nothing more than a lowly flack, he bellowed.

"Let's go outside and settle this right now," he said, raising his fists like a boxer. I wondered if maybe he'd seen too many of his bad movies lately. I demurred. He was a lot bigger than me and I wasn't angry enough or drunk enough to take him on.

Then he delivered a classic line. "Lennie Shapiro [our client] is one of my best friends. We play tennis every week. I'll see to it that you never work for him again."

For several days I walked on egg shells waiting to be summonsed by Lennie, ready with my explanation should he bring up the subject. The days went by and I heard nothing. Maybe the producer changed his mind or perhaps Lennie recognized him as a blowhard and ignored the whole deal. At any rate, we did work for Shapiro again the following year and he and I have remained on the best of terms. We even played tennis together at a 1994 Cannes tennis tournament and I have never seen that producer again.

***

When actor/director Mario Van Peebles and his father, actor/director Melvin Van Peebles, came to Cannes in 1991, Melvin marveled that it was all of 20 years since we last worked together in Paris when he was directing "The Watermelon Man" and from then on he introduced me to everyone he met as his "old high school buddy".

Melvin was one of the first black members of the Directors Guild of America. Mario has successfully followed his pioneering dad.

They enjoyed themselves in Cannes until one particular evening. I'd been invited to a party and when they heard, they asked if they could go too. I assured them it would be no problem and arranged to meet them there. To my horror, the party had been overbooked and in spite of all my pleadings, I couldn't get them in.

Lines of anger marched across Melvin's face when I told him.

"That's okay," he said. "We're used to this kind of thing. When you're black a lot of doors get slammed in your face."

I was engulfed by a flush of embarrassment.

"No, no, it's nothing like that. Nothing to do with your color. They are just full," I stammered.

"Look, we understand. It's not your fault. Don't worry about us. We'll just have to find something else to do this evening," he replied.

They saw the look of misery on my face and could contain themselves no longer. They both burst out laughing and Melvin put his arm round my shoulders.

"Gotcha!" he yelled with glee.

I caught them at another party later on. They were having a great time.

***

That same year I also had to look after the statuesque beauty, Birgitte Nielsen. She was in town with her then boyfriend, football player Mark Gastineau, to promote a film she was planning to make. She would be a sort of James Bond with boobs. I set up a press conference and a number of individual interviews. We held a cocktail party on board Christopher Lambert's yacht. Lou Ferrigno (The Incredible Hulk) also joined us. I'm an average built guy—five nine on a good day, 160 pounds, but as I stood there surrounded by these giants I felt like a shrub in a redwood forest.

On Birgitte's last day in Cannes we held a lunch in her honor at the Carlton Beach. Once everyone was settled I walked over to the nearby jetty and whispered to one of the paparazzi who are always hanging around that Birgitte was lunching on the beach. Sure enough, within three minutes photographers were buzzing around our table like bees round honey. As lunch ended I climbed the stairs to the Croisette where our limo was waiting and told another group of photographers that Ms. Nielsen would shortly be appearing. These photographers were really no good to me from a publicity point of view. I had no way of tracking where their photos would appear, if they appeared anywhere. This whole exercise was designed to make Birgitte Nielsen feel important. Sure enough, some 50 photographers mobbed us as we emerged from the restaurant. Though I had summonsed them (discreetly) I now pushed them aside.

"Sorry, no pictures, no time," I declared officiously as I ushered our star into her waiting limo as if she were visiting royalty.

Unfortunately, this was another one of those films that never got made, so this exercise turned out to be one of futility. Birgitte had been paid part of her salary in advance (I believe it was $100,000) as this was the only way she'd agree to do the film. She had, however, neglected to inform the producers about one tiny detail. She was three months pregnant! By the time they were ready to start shooting a month later, she was showing. As this was a very physical role there was no way she could do the part. I think she finally returned the money, after a number of legal threats.

***

Perhaps the most blatant bullshit session occurred at the 1994 Cannes Festival. I was working with a producer who was preparing to shoot a film in Eastern Europe.

I set up a meeting with a reporter from a small trade paper and, as I sat in on the interview, I realized that I was listening to an incredible, breakthrough news story. The producer casually explained to the journalist that he would be shooting a movie with no film in the camera. It would be the first picture ever shot digitally from start to finish. Instead of rushing exposed film to a lab somewhere, then having the dailies shipped back to the location, everything would be recorded on a sophisticated computer disc, uploaded to a satellite and then downloaded to a computer company in Hollywood. They would work on it that day (overnight in Europe) and return it via satellite to the location the next morning. No film to be lost or damaged. The movie would not be transferred to 35mm film until all the special effects, sound and music had been mixed. He would end up with a pristine print that had not been worked on at all. The producer explained that he owned the rights to this process together with two major Hollywood companies. One of them had developed the special camera. The other had worked on the software.

I told the producer that this major news event should not have been released in this way, but should have been the subject of a press conference. It was too late for that, so I organized a lunch at the Martinez Beach the following day with a writer from The Hollywood Reporter.

As I'd hoped, it was a major piece on the paper's front page and everyone was talking about it. The producer left that day to scout locations and I breathed a happy sigh, having been able to salvage this news break.

Then the shit hit the fan. One of the companies named said they had never heard of my producer. It was, however, true that they were working on this process. It was highly secret and they would not be ready to announce it for another year at least, let alone shoot a film with it. Apparently the producer had heard about it from a friend in the industry and decided to appropriate the technique as his own.

***

Sometimes Cannes can be hazardous to your health. From time to time my duties include rolling up my sleeves and doing some heavy-duty work. Advertising and billboards are never ready in time for the start of the festival and the only way to make sure things happen is to take care of them yourself. In this particular case I was handling a very heavy poster, set in a metal frame and with a wood backing. It was for a horror film and my client needed it in his suite. As I was carrying it across the lobby of the Carlton Hotel a friend stopped me and remarked on the realistic artwork.

"That's a great looking one-sheet. How did you get that blood effect?" he asked.

I looked at the lurid poster that had blood slowly trickling down the face of a corpse. It was my blood. I had cut my finger on the frame.

Later I jokingly told the client, "Look, I'll work all night for you, but I draw the line at blood!"

Cannes can be hazardous in more ways than one. Not a year goes by without my being told by someone that they've been robbed, mugged or otherwise taken advantage of.

If you rent a motor scooter I can almost guarantee that it will be stolen. I exaggerate not. In 1991 a producer friend had two rented scooters stolen on successive days. Computers are "evacuated" from hotel suites with the regularity of Exlax. My own laptop was stolen from my hotel in 2006. Fortunately it was near the end of the festival and I had emailed all the stories I would send out. Everything else was backed up on an office hard drive in Los Angeles. One friend, who rented the same apartment every year, was packed and ready to leave at the end of the festival. A burglar broke into the apartment and took all the suitcases, which were lined up in the hallway, no doubt grateful for my friend's tidy habits.

One evening I had dinner with another friend, a sales executive named Larry Meyers. Afterwards we walked slowly back along the Croisette, enjoying the warm evening air. We parted company at the apartment building where I was staying and he walked on towards his hotel. Moments later he was approached by a young male prostitute. Larry politely declined his offer and went on his way without looking back. Before he knew it the young man had jumped him and grabbed his wallet. Now, Larry is a mere four foot nine inches tall so there wasn't much he could do about it, but he was not happy. He came knocking at my door, roped in a couple more friends and together we went looking for the perp. We never did find him, but the following day Larry saw him. He found a gendarme, explained the situation, but instead of

OF KINGS AND QUEENS AND MOVIE STARS

an arrest got a Gallic shoulder shrug from the cop.

Cannes isn't always so dangerous; only at festival time. The influx of foreigners seems to bring every petty criminal in Europe to this resort.

Particularly insidious are the gangs of gypsy children that roam the streets. Their tactics are so obvious that it is amazing they ever steal anything, but they do. They will surround you, shouting, bumping and shoving. While you're distracted, one of them will pick your pocket, give it to a second child who passes it on to a third. One of them will carry a newspaper draped over his or her arm, which they use as a cover to hide their stolen goods. Even if you didn't know what was going on, that strangely draped newspaper would surely alert the most naive festivalgoer.

When they approach me I yell at them in a deep voice and wave my arms in a threatening manner. They make fun of me, but they keep their distance. I don't want to jinx future trips to Cannes, but they haven't got to me yet.

***

Some encounters in Cannes can be enjoyable. One year I attended a cocktail party given by Gaumont on the roof of the Grand Hotel. The place was packed and after I had made the rounds, making small talk with friends and acquaintances, I started down the stairs, falling into step with a beautiful French girl in her early twenties. She was friendly and I asked her out to dinner.

"I am spending this evening with friends but would be happy to go out with you some other time," she said.

"How about dinner tomorrow," I persisted.

She accepted and the following evening I took her to one of the better restaurants in town. We returned to the Carlton Hotel, where I was staying. I told her that I had to call my office in Los Angeles. She could have a coffee on the Carlton Terrace while I was on the phone or come to my room.

"I would prefer to come to your room. It is awkward for a girl to be alone on the Terrace at night."

I understood, of course, and with no lecherous thoughts on my mind, took her upstairs. However, once we were in the room and I was on the phone, she lay on her back on the bed and became extremely desirable.

I nibbled at her ear as I talked to my secretary 6,000 miles away about delivery dates and advertising schedules. By the time I was off the phone I was thoroughly aroused. As I moved in for a more serious encounter the girl put up her hand.

"I am sorry, but if you want to make love to me you will have to pay," she said, to my astonishment.

"You're a hooker."

"A girl has to make a living."

By this time I was too turned on to back down. This was many years after my failed encounter with a prostitute in Munich and I wasn't going to allow a sense of phony machismo spoil my evening."

"How much?"

"One hundred dollars."

"I don't have that much cash on me. I'll give you half now and the rest tomorrow and for that money you'll have to spend the night. It's too late for you to get any other clients tonight anyway."

She agreed to my terms and we enjoyed a night of inventive amorous adventure. The following morning I arranged to meet her on the Carlton Beach after I'd had a chance to go to the bank. I found her lying oiled and topless on the wooden decking of the Carlton pier. I suggested that we complete our transaction in a more private setting. She agreed and, after she had pulled on some clothing, we crossed the street. I gave her the money in a quiet corner of the hotel.

After she had safely tucked the money away she looked at me strangely.

"You know, I never for one minute expected you to give me the rest of the money. I thank you very much."

"A deal's a deal, whoever it's with." I told her.

***

Cannes of 1995 was the year of waiting for Tony Curtis. He was scheduled to be in town for a few days to promote the film "The Continuing Adventures of Reptile Man," due to start filming later that year.

I had been hired to handle Tony on this, his eighth visit to Cannes over the course of his long and illustrious career. Unfortunately he was not staying in town but aboard the yacht of a wealthy friend. I say "unfortunately" because the yacht was unable to find a mooring at either of Cannes' two harbors. Which meant I never knew where he was. We would send a limo out to pick him up, only he'd be some place else.

That first morning he arrived an hour late at the Majestic Hotel for a press breakfast with the trade papers. This was just as well as most of the reporters who had promised to be there hadn't shown up at all. I spent that hour most constructively, rounding up any journalists or photographers I could find. Tony arrived majestically at the Majestic just as I'd managed to fill up the room.

He disappeared for lunch and returned an hour and a half late for a slate of afternoon television interviews by the Majestic pool. With him was his tall, blonde and extremely well endowed girlfriend, Jill.

The following morning was even more nerve-wracking. Tony had recently written his autobiography and I'd arranged for him to do a book signing at the English Book Shop on the rue Bivouac Napoleon. The store owners had been promoting the hell out of the visit for a couple of days. We had local live radio covering it and I had alerted the rest of the media. Of course he was late. At first his boat was going to dock at Antibes to the east, then at St. Tropez to the west. It ended up sailing into the Cannes bay more than an hour late. I got the word that he would be arriving by dinghy at the Majestic pier. I rushed down there, followed by a couple of bodyguards I'd hired. Eventually we spotted his dinghy approaching. Tony was standing at the helm saluting like a fucking admiral. He was dressed in a white jacket, white tee shirt, white shorts and sandals and was wearing some medal that the French government had given him. The bodyguards rushed him off the pier preceded by back pedaling photographers. It was simpler to walk to the book shop than get into a car.

"I thought you said this place was round the corner," said Tony plaintively as we hurried along.

"It is. I just didn't say which corner," I replied.

People recognized him instantly, and cries of "Tony! Tony!" followed us. Finally we did turn that corner. Rue Bivouac Napoleon is a narrow street and it was blocked from one end to the other with spectators, photographers and television cameramen. I got left behind as we battled our way through the mob at the shop's entrance. One of the bodyguards noticed and picked me up like a small child, lifting me over the crowd and lowering me gently inside the doorway. The pressure was enormous, with cameramen jostling their equipment and the people who had bought books struggling to get to the table where Tony Curtis had been settled. I was afraid that spectators peering through the plate glass window would be shoved through it by the crowd behind them. Literally battling the photographers to make room for customers we eventually got some order, but not before Tony had retreated into a back room in a huff. I think he eventually signed about a hundred copies of his book. Outside, a limo was waiting, but instead of stepping straight into it, Tony waded right into the mob, shaking every hand that was offered. He made a point of talking to and posing with the policemen who were now controlling the crowd.

Finally we were in the car, which inched its way forward. Even after we had turned a couple of corners there were still people standing waving and smiling.

"That whole thing was really fucked up," said Tony.

"No it wasn't. That was chaos and you loved it," I replied.

He thought for a moment then nodded. "You're right, you know. All these years I've been coming here and each time they seem to love me more and more. I like this place." he settled back into his seat, a smile on his face.

On the third day Tony and Jill moved into the Carlton Hotel driving in, late of course, from St. Tropez. I'd scheduled a live interview that evening on France's number one rated television show. It was broadcast every evening during the festival from a stage specially built on the beach across from the Martinez Hotel.

Once I knew Tony was in his room I called up and told him that they needed him at the Martinez at 7.20. He was slotted in for the prime eight o'clock interview. I would meet him in the Carlton lobby. To my astonishment he started yelling, "I'll say when I'm going to be there. Maybe I'll be down at 7.30, maybe eight, maybe not at all. In any case it'll be when I decide, not when somebody tells me."

"Whatever," I said, sounding calm but feeling like shit. "In any case I'll be waiting downstairs."

"You don't have to wait," he replied, already feeling bad for his outburst.

"I'll be here."

That was one very long wait. I had a car waiting downstairs, although it would normally be a five-minute walk. I was in telephone contact with the nervous producers, assuring them that he would show but not really being sure at all.

At ten minutes to eight a smiling and relaxed Tony Curtis, with Jill in plunging neckline on his arm, emerged from the elevator. He immediately apologized to me for "talking to you like a dog" and explained that he thought he had lost their passports and was in a panic when I called. The passports had been found and all was well. He stopped to sign autographs and chat with his admirers. I told him we really had to hurry.

"Don't worry," he said. "When we get there they'll be so relieved they'll be falling over themselves to be nice."

He was right. We were rushed across the street to the stage. They wanted to take him to the make-up room, but he refused, saying he never wore make-up. They wanted to give him an earpiece so that he could get a translation of the questions they would be asking him. He refused that too, though he didn't understand a word of French.

Well, he went on and he was terrific. They asked him their questions and he did his shtick, which had nothing to do with the subject being discussed, and the live audience loved it.

Later he went out into the street and milked the crowd, posing with a couple of kids in wheelchairs. He was late for dinner, of course, but he didn't care. He was with his fans and they loved him.

Jill loves him too, for she is now his wife.

***

REVOLUTION!

Nineteen-sixty-eight was a watershed year throughout the world. In America, Robert Kennedy and Dr. Martin Luther King achieved premature martyrdom, while in Europe, times they were a changin' too.

In the spring of that year France was going through les événements, the events, a euphemistic Gallic phrase for revolution.

I had just returned to Paris after two years of living in Munich and Brussels and had found an apartment in Meudon, a picturesque village southwest of the city. Ironically it was in Meudon that the revolution (we will avoid euphemisms in these pages) started. Scientists at the Meudon Observatory went on strike, their action revealing the canker of dissatisfaction that was festering in the hearts of Frenchmen. Soon this hitherto unknown little group was joined by students and workers throughout the nation, a dangerous combination in the minds of the Gaullist government.

The students took to the streets, overturned cars, ripped up paving stones, started fires, smashed windows and did battle with les flics, the cops, and the CRS, the riot police. The workers closed everything down. No garbage removal, no public transport, no planes, no gas.

It was nothing less than a Communist revolution and came very close to succeeding.

Meanwhile, life goes on and I had a job to do. I'd been assigned to go to the Karlovy Vary Film Festival in Czechoslovakia. With no flights out of Paris, the only way I could make it was to drive to the Belgian border and work my way from there. Fortunately I had half a tank of gas. I calculated that if I conserved gas by driving at a steady 40 mph I might make it the 150 miles to the border. Believe me, it's very hard to drive on an empty autoroute at that speed.

I'd been driving on fumes for 20 miles when I came to the first Belgian gas station. In those days the Belgian roads were terrible, no express roads until you reached the outskirts of Brussels. So, now that I had the gas I was still forced to drive at annoyingly slow speeds. As I reached the outskirts of the

OF KINGS AND QUEENS AND MOVIE STARS

city there was a loud bang. I'd had a blow out. I trundled the car into a service station and offered to pay double their normal charge if they could change my tire in five minutes. It was like a pit stop and I was out of there in four.

A plane ticket was waiting for me at Columbia Pictures' Brussels office on the Rue Royale. I had time to grab the ticket, gulp down a Coke and battle my way to the airport. I made my flight to Germany with seconds to spare. In Munich I picked up a new Mercedes rental and for the first time was able to relax. I made the leisurely drive to the Czech border and beyond to the lovely medieval spa town of Karlovy Vary (Carlsbad when it belonged to the Germans).

The change in attitude was a shock because another, quieter revolution was going on here. After 23 years of Communist rule, the Czech government, under the leadership of Alexander Dubcek, was turning to the West. This was known as the Spring of Dubcek.

I'd traveled from a country trying to turn to Communism, to a nation that was attempting to loosen those same shackles. From a people disenchanted I had come to a land of joy.

"We are free, we are free," they would cry out to each other and to any foreigner who cared to listen.

The Czech officials could not do enough for us. They overwhelmed us with their bonhomie. Local people demanded to learn about life in the West, the lifestyle they were convinced would soon be theirs.

Karlovy Vary was a lovely old town, locked in time. Patients at the various clinics would walk the streets sipping at the city's famous spa water through special cups with spouts.

Everyone was in a joyous mood, even the visitors. In the hotel elevator a man said to me for no apparent reason, "Hello, young man. My name's Tony Curtis. What's yours?" This struck me as a bit silly. Of course he was Tony Curtis. Anybody knew that. Curtis was there with his young bride of a few weeks. At a formal dinner party that evening he stood up and announced loudly, "My bride and I are leaving you now to go to bed because that is what newlyweds do. Good night." I felt embarrassed for his wife. It would be 27 years before our paths crossed again. By this time he was getting ready to take another wife.

I left Czechoslovakia the following week feeling good with the world.

Two months later Soviet tanks rolled into the country and the candle of freedom flickered and died.

I returned to Karlovy Vary in 1970 and found a different world. The local officials with whom I'd become friends two years earlier had disappeared. In their stead were dour faced apparatchiks. Joy had been replaced by blank faces of despair.

The film I was representing at this festival was "Guess Who's Coming to Dinner", directed by Stanley Kramer. Catherine Houghton, who played the daughter of Spencer Tracy and Katherine Hepburn in the movie was in Karlovy Vary too. Catherine is actually Hepburn's niece.

She told me a poignant story about the making of this film. Towards the end of the production Spencer Tracy's character gave a powerful speech in which he declared his lifelong love for his wife. The actors and the entire film crew were reduced to tears, for these were no mere lines he was delivering. Katherine Hepburn was, of course, the great love in his real life and everyone, including Tracy, knew that he was dying. A few days after production ended he did indeed pass away. Rarely has someone been able to leave such a powerful epitaph for himself.

Exactly 30 years after that first visit to Prague, in the spring of 1998, I was back there again, working on a Jack the Ripper movie called "Love Lies Bleeding." What a difference! The Communists had been gone for several years by this time and the city had blossomed into one of the most beautiful and vibrant in all of Europe. We filmed all over the ancient city, which was supposed to depict Victorian London. One of the stars was the notoriously difficult Faye Dunaway. She certainly lived up to her reputation, reducing the hair and make-up ladies to tears with her tirades and causing endless delays on the set with her "suggestions." Strangely enough, however, I had no problems with her. On her last day on the set I brought in a television crew so that I could do a video interview with her. She told me that she would do it when filming had finished. The crew and I waited around until one thirty a.m. I was sure it was a waste of time because she was scheduled to leave her hotel four hours later to catch a flight to New York. Well, she did it. True, she fussed around, telling us where we should put the camera, how high it should be, telling the gaffer what lights to use and where they should be, even telling me where to sit. But once that camera started rolling she was the complete professional and gave an excellent interview.

***

OF KINGS AND QUEENS AND MOVIE STARS

Morpurgo (rt) with the Duke and Duchess of Windsor and their equerry at Paris premiere of "A King's Story."

LEONARD MORPURGO

Anthony Mann at the London premiere of "El Cid."

OF KINGS AND QUEENS AND MOVIE STARS

Trailing behind Italian actress Claudia Cardinale and French actor Jean Sorel at the Venice Film Festival.

LEONARD MORPURGO

Chatting with Italian movie star Monica Vitti on board the S.S. Italia somewhere on the Mediterranean.

OF KINGS AND QUEENS AND MOVIE STARS

Morpurgo watches as Sam Spiegel is presented to Queen Elizabeth at the world premiere of "Lawrence of Arabia."

LEONARD MORPURGO

Morpurgo waits to be presented to Queen Fabiola at the Belgian premiere of "A Man for All Seasons." King Baudoin is to the Queen's left.

OF KINGS AND QUEENS AND MOVIE STARS

With Charlton Heston at the premiere of "El Cid."

LEONARD MORPURGO

Morpurgo watches Leslie Caron, Woody Allen and Ursula Andress at the Royal Film Performance of "Born Free" in London.

OF KINGS AND QUEENS AND MOVIE STARS

Promoting "Lawrence of Arabia" with Anthony Quinn.

LEONARD MORPURGO

With Austrian actress Senta Berger and George Segal and his wife at the Lido de Paris.

"Interviewing" Oliver Reed at a failed Zurich press conference for "Oliver."

OF KINGS AND QUEENS AND MOVIE STARS

Jack Nicholson gets interviewed in Munich for "Five Easy Pieces."

LEONARD MORPURGO

Escorting Jane Fonda and her husband Roger Vadim at the Berlin Film Festival.

OF KINGS AND QUEENS AND MOVIE STARS

Richard "Jaws" Kiel "strangles" Morpurgo and his son Benjamin at the Cannes Film Festival.

Morpurgo goes over a press interview schedule with director Arthur Penn on the Paris set of "Target."

LEONARD MORPURGO

*With producer David Brown and star Matt Dillon
at Dallas-Fort Worth Airport during filming of "Target."*

OF KINGS AND QUEENS AND MOVIE STARS

Accompanying Elliot Gould at a festival in Palermo, Italy.

LEONARD MORPURGO

With famed director William Wyler in Italy.

OF KINGS AND QUEENS AND MOVIE STARS

Greeting Eli Wallach and his wife Ann Jackson at Munich Airport.

LEONARD MORPURGO

With young Mark Lester at the Vienna premiere of "Oliver."

OF KINGS AND QUEENS AND MOVIE STARS

With Senta Berger in Copenhagen.

LEONARD MORPURGO

Talking to Peter Sellers and his wife Lynne Frederick at the Cannes Film Festival screening of "Being There."

OF KINGS AND QUEENS AND MOVIE STARS

Readying Michael York for a television interview at the Martinez Hotel in Cannes.

LEONARD MORPURGO

With the Casino Royale girls at the Brussels Motor Show.

OF KINGS AND QUEENS AND MOVIE STARS

With the Killer Girls from the "Matt Helm" movies in Munich, Germany.

LEONARD MORPURGO

Arriving at Copenhagen Airport with Leslie Caron for the Danish premiere of "The L-Shaped Room."

OF KINGS AND QUEENS AND MOVIE STARS

With Gene Hackman on the Paris set of "Target."

LEONARD MORPURGO

l. to r. David Lewin, British newspaper columnist, Peter Sellers and Morpurgo at the famed Hotel du Cap, Cap d'Antibes, France.

OF KINGS AND QUEENS AND MOVIE STARS

With Jon Voight in Tokyo, promoting "Table for Five" in 1982.

LEONARD MORPURGO

Photo: Craig T. Mathew/Mathew Imaging

With Jon Voight at the Beverly Hilton Hotel in 2007.

OF KINGS AND QUEENS AND MOVIE STARS

Dancing with Ann-Margret in Stockholm, Sweden in 1963 after the local premiere of "Bye Bye Birdie."

With actress Erika Anderson and a sheet in a Rome hotel.

LEONARD MORPURGO

Morpurgo with Ari Sandel, winner of the 2006 Oscar® for Best Live Action Short ("West Bank Story").

OF KINGS AND QUEENS AND MOVIE STARS

Photo: Craig T. Mathew/Mathew Imaging

Lunching with Sienna Miller in Beverly Hills in 2007 in promotion for "Factory Girl."

LEONARD MORPURGO

With documentary filmmakers Cecilia Peck and Barbara Koppel ("Shut Up And Sing") in Monaco 2007.

With 2005 Oscar® winner Paul Haggis ("Crash") and Murray Weissman.

OF KINGS AND QUEENS AND MOVIE STARS 113

AWAY FROM IT ALL

Karlovy Vary may be a different kind of place for someone who grew up in Western Europe, but it's still a fairly large town with most of the conveniences that come with it. Sometimes movie premieres are arranged away from city lights and these events can be fun, though logistic nightmares.

In the winter of 1970 Avoriaz was a sparkling new ski resort nestled high in the French Alps with a cinema and a lot of empty hotel rooms. It could use a good promotion.

At the same time, Columbia Pictures had a romantic comedy titled "Bob & Carol & Ted & Alice". The film was highly risqué for the era. It could use a good promotion.

Partners!

Why don't we hold the film's European premiere in Avoriaz, someone suggested. The city fathers were delighted at the idea and were ready to give us excellent price breaks in return for all that publicity.

We contacted French celebrities and European media and offered them a movie and a long weekend in the Alps. The response was excellent. People like to be the first to try anything so that they can casually boast about it to their friends. Celebrities are no exception.

Brigitte Bardot, mega pop star Johnny Halliday and the real Papillon, were among the French headline makers who accepted. Papillon was a famous criminal who had been sent to Devil's Island, had escaped more than once and had written a hugely successful book about his experiences. Three years later Steve McQueen would play him in the movie of the same name.

Of the film's four stars—Robert Culp, Dyan Cannon, Elliot Gould and Natalie Wood, only Natalie made the trip, accompanied by her husband, Richard Gregson. This was a marriage sandwiched in between her two weddings to Robert Wagner.

How to get these 200 or so people the 400 miles from Paris to Avoriaz?

Simple! We rented an entire train that took us from the Gare de l'Est to Geneva; in and out of Switzerland before you could say "Voila!" a fleet of buses to the town of Morzine in the Haute Savoie; the téléphérique up the mountainside to Avoriaz; sleighs to our hotel. No problem.

This was a wonderfully relaxing couple of days. Somehow, the brisk mountain air, fresh snow and the clean new town with no automobiles, put everyone in a good mood.

One potentially dangerous encounter turned into a love fest. In addition to Papillon we had invited the Préfet de Police who had put him away. Nervously I brought Papillon over to where his one-time nemesis was standing. Instead of insults there were broad smiles. Soon they were swapping reminiscences over an aperitif. On reflection, this was understandable. They owed their fame to each other and Papillon wouldn't have been able to write his book and become rich without Monsieur le Préfet.

Columbia did well out of this off-the-beaten-track premiere. "Bob & Carol & Ted & Alice" became a big hit. Its poster, daringly showing the four stars together in one bed, has become a collectors' item.

Avoriaz also got its money's worth. For many years it has been the site of the world's premiere fantasy and science fiction film festival, run by the same group that organizes the Deauville Film Festival in the north of France. With a paucity of good films in the genre, however, the Avoriaz Festival ended in 1993 and now is run by a different group and has a different name.

I didn't have to travel quite so far for the premiere of "Waterloo," the epic story of Napoleon's great defeat. The film was screened in Brussels and a luncheon was held the following day at a rustic restaurant outside town—right in the middle of the Waterloo battlefield itself. The site has been preserved exactly as it was on June 18, 1815. Even the building housing the restaurant was original.

For various reasons the film, which starred Rod Steiger in the title role, had not been shot there, but at a site in eastern Europe. Having just seen the film, it was a treat for all the press at the lunch to see the amazing resemblance between the film battle site and the real thing. Every hill, every copse, every field was identical. A most impressive piece of location finding.

Until January 17, 1994 I had a souvenir of that party back in 1971—a beer glass engraved with an "N" for Napoleon. The glass was one of many possessions that failed to survive the big Northridge earthquake on that date (My home is just three miles from the epicenter).

Perhaps the most glamorous and unusual venue for a screening was the site chosen for the world premiere of the Italian film "Amore Mio, Aiuto Mi!" ("Help Me, Darling!"), starring the gorgeous Monica Vitti and Italy's leading comic actor, Alberto Sordi.

Much of the film's action takes place on board the S.S. Italia, which was the flagship of Italy's cruise line and that is where we held the premiere. Once again we rented a train, or at least several carriages, and rode from Rome to Naples, where the ship was docked. Once we'd all been shown to our allocated cabins we headed out into the Mediterranean for a two-day cruise—north to Nice, then back to Naples.

The film was screened in two sessions that evening following the sort of multi-course meal you find only on cruise ships, especially Italian cruise ships.

I was hardly able to button my pants when I left the ship the following morning upon docking at Nice. My work was done and I would be flying back to Paris that evening. Meanwhile, I felt deliciously guilty idling this workday on the beach and basking in the sun of the Cote d'Azur, waiting for the cruise food to digest.

***

WE SHOT J.R.

Though most of my work has been in motion pictures, I've occasionally ventured into television publicity. The most notable of these television shows was "Dallas", the first of the prime time soaps.

I'd been hired by Lorimar to handle international motion picture publicity, but members of the foreign press were always asking for interviews with stars of the studio's television shows, so I gradually became more involved in that area. As well as "Dallas," Lorimar was producing such long-running hits as "The Waltons," "Eight Is Enough" and "Knots Landing."

It was "Dallas," however, that grabbed all the attention.

As excitement about the series spread across the planet like an infectious disease, requests for interviews with the cast grew to frenzied proportions. The main interest focused on Larry Hagman, the infamous J.R.; Patrick Duffy, who portrayed his good brother Bobby; and Victoria Principal, as Bobby's beautiful wife.

Usually it was my job to court the media, asking them if they could possibly interview so-and-so or do a photo session with such-and-such an actor. I discovered for the first time in my career that, though movies might be more glamorous and prestigious, television was infinitely more powerful a medium.

I recall one sad and nostalgic photo session I arranged for Patrick Duffy and a German magazine. "Dallas" was shot on a couple of sound stages at the then MGM Studios. (It later became known as Lorimar Studios, Lorimar Telepictures, Columbia Warner, Columbia Studios and, at the time of writing, Sony Pictures Entertainment Studios.) We arranged to do the shoot on the backlot, just west of the main studio. We walked through crumbling "New York" streets and past the lamppost that Gene Kelly had swung on in "Singin' in the Rain". This film had impressed me greatly when I was a youngster living in England and I remember singing and dancing down Regent Street in London's West End after seeing it. I thought I was Gene Kelly. Now, here I was on that very street. Two weeks later the

OF KINGS AND QUEENS AND MOVIE STARS

entire backlot was razed and replaced by a housing development. That's progress for you.

Larry Hagman was a fun interview. An anti-smoking nut, he always carried half a dozen or more small, battery-run fans with him. At lunch he would place them all around the table to keep away cigarette smoke from other tables. Times have changed since then, of course. At first, restaurants were forced to designate non-smoking areas. Currently, smoking is banned totally in Los Angeles restaurants. Larry's campaign seems to have worked.

He had an eclectic collection of hats, many of them sent to him from fans around the world. One cap took his air clearing mania a step further, with a small whirring propeller embedded in the front.

I had to be sparing in my request for interviews from the "Dallas" stars as I didn't want to wear out my welcome. During the season, they worked 14 to 16 hour days on the set and also had to contend with interviews by the domestic American press.

The pressure grew as the series' 1979-80 season drew to a close. As I wrote in an article at the time: "While thousands are running to their analysts (or their bookmakers in the United Kingdom) the greatest anxiety in the world today appears not to be the Afghanistan crisis, the hostages in Iran, or the boycott of the Moscow Olympics, but the fate of that unprincipled J.R. Ewing."

When the season ended with the shooting of J.R., a new phrase entered the entertainment lexicon— "Who shot J.R.?" My phone rang non-stop, not only with calls from the locally based international press but from almost every country in the world. Writers begged me for the answer to that pervasive question. One journalist even offered me a car as a bribe if I could tell him exclusively who had done the dirty deed. The truth is, I didn't know and didn't want to know. I did make an educated guess, which I kept to myself, and I turned out to be right.

So desperate were the media to get an interview, any interview, that I was interviewed several times myself, including a live radio show in Australia. The respected British television journalist, Patrick Gibbs, writing for the Daily Telegraph, called it the greatest publicity campaign since the days of Barnum and Bailey or Mike Todd. A good publicity man works in a way to make it appear that he doesn't exist, that the publicity is organic, a natural phenomenon rising out of the greatness of a star or a show. When I disowned any authorship for the publicity, explaining that it was like a snowball rolling downhill and growing all by itself, he replied sarcastically, "Yeah, right!"

Someone broke into the "Dallas" production office and stole the final episode script. This didn't help them as several versions of the script were not only written but filmed, so even the cast members were in the dark. A cynical press accused us of staging this burglary as a publicity stunt. We didn't, simply because we didn't need to. The print of the final episode destined for the U.K. was taken by armed security guards to Los Angeles Airport the night before it was to be aired.

When the identity of the killer (Mary Crosby) was finally revealed in the fall of 1980, BBC Television opened its evening newscast with the story. Around the world, cinemas shut down for the night and restaurants closed (unless they had a TV set). Streets were empty of traffic.

Nothing lasts forever and once the world knew who had shot J.R. the show began its long, slow decline.

My job at Lorimar came about in a most fortuitous manner in 1978. I'd arrived in California some four years earlier, after my public relations business in Paris had gone down the tubes. Disillusioned by the swollen egos and broken promises of the entertainment industry, I came to the United States determined to get into a different line of work. I had a wife and 18-month old twin sons to support and needed a less fickle mistress than motion pictures. It wasn't as easy as I'd supposed. Living in San Diego, I was in and out of a variety of jobs. I started a public relations and advertising company but found that retail clients paid no quicker than entertainment clients.

Out of the blue I received a call from Bobby Meyers who was President of Lorimar Pictures International. Was I interested in being interviewed for the job of Director of International Advertising and Publicity at the studio? Bobby and I went way back. We had worked together at Columbia Pictures and, when he was at National General Pictures, he became the first client at my Paris agency.

I told him that I was interested with one condition. I had to have a decision from Lorimar, one way or the other, within 24 hours. Or they could stuff their job. I was bluffing with a pair of deuces and it worked. The following day I was hired.

I spent an interesting two and a half years at Lorimar. The company, which was riding high at the time, organized three "La Costa Film Weeks" over a period of four years. I was there for the last two. La Costa is a luxurious resort north of San Diego and at the time one of the owners was Merv Adelson, Chairman of Lorimar. We invited some 300 film distributors from around the world to visit the resort for five days of screenings, seminars, parties, get-togethers with Hollywood stars, and golf and tennis tournaments. They were asked to pay their own way to Los Angeles. Lorimar took care of all their other expenses. It was an event to which everyone involved looked forward. Lorimar sold its films and gained a tremendous prestige, while the distributors did good business in a vacation atmosphere.

Special events organizer, Buddy Goldberg, was brought in to coordinate these events, which were Bobby Meyers' baby. I worked closely with Buddy in putting the whole thing together. He was not an easy man to get along with. A perfectionist, with a huge ego, he was convinced that he was the only person capable of doing the job. He made life hell for his staff and I became very protective of them. So we rowed continuously. In spite of all this I liked the man and eventually we became good friends.

Other production and distribution companies in Los Angeles invited the international visitors to screenings and parties before and after our event while La Costa became too expensive for one company to sustain. In 1980 we all came together and launched the American Film Market. Bobby was named the first President of the American Film Marketing Association and Buddy Goldberg was hired as Executive Director. He continued his high-handed ways until he was eventually fired under suspicion for taking kickbacks. This was never proven and he swore to me that he'd never done anything illegal.

Buddy was devastated. It's hard for any man to lose his job but for someone of Buddy's fragile ego it was a cataclysm. He became consumed with hatred for the man he was convinced had fingered him. Now that he was no longer in a position of power most of his "friends" ignored him, so I became protective of *him*. We remained close and frequently had lunch or dinner together during this period. I've never known such an angry man.

Invariably, within five minutes he would turn on the venom, wishing the plague on the man he deemed responsible for his plight and on to his children and grandchildren. He simply could not let go. He became sick and within a short time was dead from leukemia. I'm convinced he was killed by all that negative energy.

The American Film Market has since grown to become one of the three major events in the international film market, together with Cannes and the MIFED Market in Milan every October. In recent years MIFED has disbanded and is replaced by the European Film Market in Berlin. Hundreds of companies offer their wares at the AFM and thousands of buyers trek to Los Angeles for the annual occasion.

***

TWILIGHT ZONE

One spring morning in 1992, while working at the Rogers & Cowan public relations agency, I received a call from a producer named Frank Rhodes. He asked me to attend the first screening of his movie "Sandman." He wanted me to write the film's press kit.

I arrived at the small Sunset Boulevard screening room in Hollywood to find him sitting there with three or four other people. He appeared nervous.

The film had been written and directed by a young man named Eric Woster who also starred. In addition to serving as producer, Frank had written the original story together with Eric and also co-starred.

This very low budget effort, a sub-compact of a movie, tells the story of a young auto-mechanic (Eric Woster) who rents a small house in North Hollywood with a mysterious past to it. Nearly forty years earlier the family that had been living there disappeared. Our hero discovers an evil presence in the house and also finds out that the place is a window in time. He is able to go back to 1956. When he returns to the present he becomes increasingly troubled by inner demons. His attempt at suicide is thwarted by a mysterious stranger who persuades him to fight the evil that is in the house. In the climactic scene the house bursts into flame and our hero, together with his daughter and girlfriend, is able to escape only by returning in time to the security of the fifties.

The film had a special quality and I was anxious to meet Woster, a handsome, well-built blond who seemed to have a future. He was not at the screening.

Frank Rhodes invited me for a coffee. There was something he needed to explain.

He told me that the film had been three years in the making, repeatedly delayed by budgetary constraints. The haunted house of the story was actually on Laurel Canyon Boulevard in North Hollywood and was Eric Woster's own home.

Eric had wanted to make movies since he was eight, when his Uncle Peter gave him a Super 8 movie camera for his birthday. He was an All American kid who had joined the ROTC during the Vietnam War era when he was 13. A football star in high school, he ruined his knee while playing for Montana State University, effectively ending his playing career.

Eric worked on a low budget science fiction feature with Frank Rhodes, going on to be a cameraman on commercials and music videos. Over time he bought a 35 mm camera, lighting and sound equipment and formed 58 Productions, named for the year of his birth.

In 1989 he and Frank started work on "Sandman". It is an allegory for Eric Woster's own life.

This story of a man struggling to escape his internal demons, matches Eric's own obsession with the past, particular the fifties. Frank told me over coffee that day that Eric was always trying to go to a simpler place and time through the magic of movies. He was a dreamer and "Sandman" was his dream.

His obsession changed his personality. The open, easy-going Eric became argumentative and impossible to work with. He turned to alcohol and, when that didn't help, became addicted to religion, allowing that to rule his work and life to an unhealthy degree. He wanted to weave his new religious convictions into the plot of "Sandman" over Frank's strenuous objections.

The night principal photography finished on "Sandman" Eric Woster died suddenly and alone in the very same haunted house where much of the filming had taken place. A crew member found him two days later, lying in bed with the television on and with the remote control in his hand. He was 34 years old. His death remains a mystery. "Sandman" has not been released, so far as I know. The distribution company that was handling it has gone out of business.

***

BABES!

It's ten a.m., Culver City, California. The sun is already baking the sidewalks while the smog lies on the horizon like an army blanket. I'm parked thankfully in my air-conditioned office at Lorimar struggling to find the right wording for a press release. The phone rings. A woman's soft, seductive voice tells me that she is an actress and model calling from New York and she needs my help.

"How can I help you?" I ask her.

"I want to be in movies in Hollywood," she replies.

"I'm a publicist, not a producer or casting director."

"Yes, but you know producers and casting directors, don't you?"

"Yes."

"Then you can help me."

"Who gave you my name?"

"Robin Leach. He said you were very important."

Aha! I think. Robin's been bull-shitting again.

Without making any promises, I agree to meet her when she comes to California in a couple of weeks. I get back to my press release.

Two weeks later the phone rings. It's her. We set an appointment for the following afternoon.

The next day I'm on the phone again. I do a lot of that. I look up. A vision in black is standing at the door, long dark hair draped over her shoulders, smoldering eyes burning into me, her dress clinging to her like water. I'm off the phone faster than a squirrel up a tree.

"Don't move. Stay there. Keep looking the way you look. I'll be right back."

She smiles languidly, the overhead fluorescent light fading beside the white flash of her teeth.

I'm out of my chair and loping down the corridor before she can say "hello!" I stop at the office of James B. Harris, producer/director of "Fast-Walking." The film is in pre-production. It will star James Woods. "Jim," I say. "I know you're busy, but I need your help. Now."

"What's up?"

"You're looking for a female lead for your film, right?"

"Right."

"So come to my office. There's a girl there I want you to meet. Maybe she's not right for the part. Maybe she can't act. But you would be doing me a great service if you would just say 'hi' and shake her hand."

"Sure. Happy to do it," he says, following me down the hall to where The Vision is waiting.

Jim Harris is impressed. I can tell by the way his eyes glaze over.

"You are very beautiful," he says eventually. "Unfortunately I'm looking for someone a little tougher, a little rougher. But I'm glad I had the chance to meet you."

He wishes her good luck and I squeeze his shoulder in gratitude as he leaves. Later he would hire Kay Lenz for the part.

"You do television too, don't you?" says The Vision.

"Yes, lots of television."

"Maybe there's something for me there."

I ask her if she has a head-shot with her. She produces a sheaf of photos from her bag.

"Will these do?"

I scan through them. Great stuff.

"They'll do. Take a seat. I may be a while."

I hike across to the other side of the studio. Destination: Barbara Miller, Lorimar's vice president of casting. She looks through the photos.

"Very beautiful,"

This is getting repetitive.

"I may have something for her. We're casting a movie of the week that calls for a lot of model types. Have her call me."

Elated, I return to my office. I give her the good news.

"But I don't want to be a model. I'm already a model. I want to be an actress."

"This is a role. You would be an actress playing a model."

"But I want to play another kind of role. I don't want to get type cast."

"Just get cast. Make the call and worry about the type later."

So she makes the call and gets an appointment for the following week.

I make my pitch and, yes, she'd be happy to have dinner with me.

That evening she tells me that she has found a job as a cigarette girl at the Palm restaurant on Santa Monica Boulevard. Even visions got to eat.

She drops by my office the following week on the way to her audition. I wish her good luck. We have dinner again and she's heard nothing.

I call Barbara Miller the next day.

Any decision on The Vision?

"Yes. She's very beautiful."

I knew that.

"She came over very well in the interview, warm and friendly. But when it came to reading for the part she was dead cold. No expression. She should get some acting lessons."

She was cold, colder than a polar bear's behind. Beautiful, yes. Actress, no.

"Do you want me to tell her or will you?" asks Barbara.

"I'll tell her," I say charitably. "After all, I sent her to you. It's my responsibility."

I know she's working the six to two shift at the Palm that evening. It's near my West Hollywood home, so I walk over. You're not supposed to walk in Southern California but I'm in an adventurous mood. The place is packed as usual, sawdust on the floor, air like a freighter's bilge, the decibel level off the dial.

The Vision is in a corner dispensing cigarettes from the tray she carries round her shoulders.

"We have to talk," I tell her.

She leads me to a corner where the noise has dropped to a shriek.

I tell her she didn't get the part. I tell her why. The truth is brutal.

For a moment she's silent. Then she lets out a howl that cuts through the ambient sound like a jackhammer in a monastery. Tears well, the howling grows even louder. Eaters stop eating, heads turn. The howling continues.

"I'm ruined. My whole life is destroyed. What am I going to do?" she stammers between the howls.

Assuming this is a rhetorical question, I say nothing. I stand there awkwardly, wondering what the diners think I've done to her. Hell, all I did was try to help a Vision.

I pat her shoulder, mumble something like "there, there" and make my escape, her howls following me down the street.

I never see her again. Perhaps I should have told her that the first thing an actress has to learn is rejection.

***

Ornella Muti was a beautiful and voluptuous movie star beloved in her native Italy. In 1979 she came to California to make her first American picture in her first English-speaking role. The film was "Love and Money," directed by James Toback and also starring Klaus Kinski and Ray Sharkey.

They were an interesting trio of actors. Sharkey was rude and difficult and Kinski totally impossible. He would storm out of press interviews, screaming in anger for no discernible reason, to the interviewer's astonishment. Ornella was sweet and adorable, but in her way just as difficult.

She suffered the Italian disease of "domani," being utterly incapable of arriving anywhere on time, or sometimes not arriving at all. In addition, for some reason that maybe only another woman could divine, she took her career advice from her hairdresser, with whom I had more than one contretemp. After several missed or delayed interviews and photo sessions with major American publications, I decided it was time to give her some fatherly advice.

"You may be the Queen of Italian movies, adored by your public," I told her. "Perhaps you are a huge movie star throughout Europe, but in America your name means diddlysquat. If you want to be a truly international star you have to make it here. If you want to do that you must do what I ask of you and that means showing up for press interviews."

She smiled in sweet contrition and swore that she would never miss another interview. Of course the next time I arranged a photo session she had to take her little daughter to the doctor and forgot to tell me, or maybe she just had to go to the store at the last minute.

But hey, she was cute. I forgave her.

***

OF KINGS AND QUEENS AND MOVIE STARS 127

Bo Derek definitely belongs in a chapter on babes. After all, she was the original "Ten." During my tenure at CBS Theatrical Films she was set to star in "Mistress of the Seas," directed by her husband John Derek. She was to play the role of a legendary woman buccaneer and it was going to be a wonderful, sexy, swashbuckling adventure.

Before I met her I had assumed that she was just a face and a body, a girl under the Svengali-like power of her older husband. Nothing could be further from the truth. She certainly is a beautiful woman, but she is also intelligent, self-possessed and a savvy businesswoman. She makes her own decisions.

At this time I was preparing a glossy four-color brochure touting all of CBS' current and upcoming motion pictures. As "Mistress of the Seas" had not yet started shooting we had no material to work with, so I hired an artist to design a two page spread, featuring lots of pirates battling it out on the poop deck. Bo, her shirt strategically ripped to display her magnificent bosoms, was prominently displayed. Great stuff.

Bo had right of approval of all material and had even given me 40 or 50 nude photos of herself, enlarged to 16x20 in., to help the artist in his work. In the early stages of the work she was easy to find. She was either in her office at CBS' Studio City lot or working out in the gym she'd had installed in the room next door.

Then she and John took off for Europe and elsewhere to scout locations. I sent them the final artwork for approval, but by the time it arrived they had already moved on. For the next three weeks that artwork chased them round Europe, always missing them by a day. By the time it got to them and was approved, it was too late. CBS canceled the project before it could start. The budget had grown out of sight.

***

I first met Kate Capshaw at about the same time. She was starting out as an actress after an earlier career as a schoolteacher, would you believe. Her first starring role was in CBS Theatrical Films' "Windy City", also starring John Shea.

She spent a lot of time at my Studio City office once the location filming in Chicago was over. She'd come in to look at the still photography from the film (which was part of my responsibility) or she would just stay to chat. Kate was a friendly, open and obviously very beautiful babe.

Eventually the filming finished and she returned to her home in New York with her young daughter. We continued our friendship long distance and a couple of weeks later she called to ask my advice. She was thinking of moving out to the West Coast to further her film career. What did I think of the idea?

I told her that it was the best thing she could do. I felt she had a career ahead of her and it would be easier to make connections if she lived close to where the action was.

"But then I'll have to find a place to stay," she said.

Only partly in jest, I told her that she could always move in with me.

"The only trouble is, I have just one bedroom," I said.

"Well that would be fine. My daughter and I could sleep there. But where would you sleep?" she responded.

Needless to say, she didn't follow through on my munificent offer, but did move out to Los Angeles, with her daughter, a short time later.

Kate Capshaw went on to star in a number of movies and today she's Mrs. Steven Spielberg,. So I guess it was a pretty good career move.

***

We all remember certain of our birthday parties. One that sticks in my memory was in 1966. It was a warm November evening at the Hotel de Paris in Monte Carlo, a welcome break from the cold drizzle of Munich, where I was living at that time.

What a party it was! Friends of mine showed up from every country in Europe. Prince Rainier and Princess Grace were there and so was that most gorgeous of babes, Claudia Cardinale.

This is all true—but not the whole truth. Yes, it was my birthday, but that wasn't the reason for the party. We'd organized a charity premiere in Monaco for "The Professionals", a wonderful western starring Burt Lancaster, Lee Marvin and Claudia Cardinale. I had invited key press from the major European countries and most of them were indeed my friends.

When the four-man German television crew learned that this was my

OF KINGS AND QUEENS AND MOVIE STARS

birthday they marched over to my table, clicked their heels, bowed and said "viel Glück zum Geburtstag" in unison. Rainier and Grace offered me their congratulations and Claudia gave me a big birthday kiss.

***

This next item may not be much about babes, but it does follow on from the previous paragraph.

I was back in Monte Carlo in 2007, this time as a guest of the Monaco Music Film Festival. The organizers, who were new to the festival game, wanted me to observe and to advise them on how they could improve the event in future years.

While there I became friends with Barbara Koppel and Cecilia Peck, producers of the documentary about the Dixie Chicks, "Shut Up and Sing." Cecilia, who had spent her childhood summers in the area, took us one evening to an Italian restaurant on one of the town's hillside streets, a place she had frequently been to with her father, Gregory Peck and his buddies, including Frank Sinatra. The restaurant owner was delighted to find out who she was and proudly showed us a photo of Peck and Sinatra adorning one of the restaurant walls. As the wine flowed and the evening became night, the conversation drifted to golf.

"You play?" the proprietor asked me.

"Sure, some," I replied.

"Okay let's go hit a few," he replied, to my astonishment.

"What! It's nearly midnight and we're on a mountainside in the middle of a city. And you want to play golf?"

"No problem. Follow me."

He led me outside, handed me a club and laid a square of Astroturf on the street. He produced a plastic bag and emptied its contents on the ground. They were champagne corks.

"See if you can hit that light," he said, pointing to a light pole about 150 yards down the narrow street. I swung at the cork, which traveled reasonably far, but missed the light.

"Now I try," he said. Fortunately he didn't get any closer than I had, so my honor remained intact. We took alternate strokes, never getting any closer to the lamp, but managing to hit a few apartment windows and parked cars. The taxi I had ordered pulled up and the driver watched us for a while.

"Nice form," the driver told me, as our group piled into his cab.

"Shut up and Sing" was the closing night film, and as I waited in the lobby, dressed in my tux, Prince Albert, the son of the late Prince Rainier and Princess Grace arrived. He was wearing a sports jacket and when he saw me he said, "My apologies, Monsieur. But I am not dressed appropriately. I've been working on my bike."

My immediate response was, "Hey man, you own this country. You can dress how you like here." Except that I never voiced that out loud. All I said was, "I'm sure that's not a problem."

He smiled and shook my hand.

***

There are all kinds of babes. There are drop dead gorgeous babes like Claudia, Ornella and The Vision and then there are special babes—like Perle Mesta.

During the fifties she was Washington's most famous party-giver and was immortalized in a Broadway show as "the hostess with the mostest". Because of her reputation as a hostess I got a terrific kick out of turning the tables and playing host to her.

One day in 1971 I received a call from Columbia's New York office. Miss Mesta would be in Paris for a few days and they wanted me to take her out to dinner. She was an important connection for our Washington lobbyist (yes, even movie studios have lobbyists).

Though she was advanced in years at this time, Perle Mesta was young in spirit and a delightful companion. We ate at the beautiful Le Doyen restaurant located in the wooded area of the Champs Elysees.

For one night I was the host with the most.

***

At the age of 19, Lynn Redgrave was an awkward babe. Tall and overweight, she had just starred in her first film, as the introverted and homely "Georgy Girl." It was a tough time for her as the youngest member of a British acting dynasty, following her father, Sir Michael and sister, Vanessa.

She had to face further pressure when she arrived at the 1966 Berlin Film Festival for the very first public showing of the film. She had never been the subject of a press junket before yet, for a couple of days, seemed to be handling it well. I had assigned a woman translator to sit in on all her interviews and Lynn bravely continued to answer the same predictable questions.

On the third day she took me to one side. "Leonard, please, please get that dyke out of my sight," she said.

Apparently, the woman, a lesbian, had mistaken Lynn for a kindred spirit and had been making passes at her. I fired the translator and took over the job myself for the duration of our visit.

Happily, Lynn grew out of her awkwardness, shed her puppy fat and even became a spokesperson for a diet company.

***

Jodie Foster has been in the public eye all her life. As the world knows, it hasn't always been a comfortable place for her.

I met up with the young actress in 1980, when, at the age of 18, she played her first adult role in Lorimar's "Carny". She portrayed a girl who runs away from an oppressive home life to work in a traveling carnival.

Jodie agreed to do a lunch interview with an important European journalist who was visiting Los Angeles. When I suggested a certain Sunset Strip restaurant, she at first demurred, saying that it was a well-known drug hang-out and that her mother wouldn't approve.

"How bad an influence can it be? It's a beautiful day and we'll be in the restaurant's garden. There won't be any drug pushing going on," I said.

So she agreed.

As we walked down the long flight of stone steps that led from Sunset Boulevard to the garden below, I saw two or three hypodermic needles lying on the ground."

"I told you so," said Jodie, giving me a withering look.

Oops!

At least the interview went well and we saw no overt drug peddling or using.

In March of the following year, John Hinckley showed his "love" for

Jodie by attempting to assassinate President Ronald Reagan—and Jodie's life changed. Although she'd temporarily given up show business at this time to study at Yale, I saw her back in Los Angeles a short time after the Hinckley incident. She was lunching with a friend on the patio of the Old World restaurant in West Hollywood.

I called out her name. She almost jumped out of her seat and for a moment I saw a look of blanched terror on her face before she recognized me and relaxed.

I'd caught a glimpse of the flip side of fame.

***

Jane Fonda, a sometime babe, is one of the world's most intriguing personalities, possibly because there are so many versions of her. She's like an artist who goes through a series of artistic periods. You know, Picasso's "blue period" and so on.

Jane had her Barbarella "bimbo" period, her anti-war activist period, her serious actress period, her fitness video period, which led to her entrepreneurial business woman period and her wife and partner of mogul Ted Turner period. As of this writing she's in her older movie star period.

I met Jane shortly after the "bimbo" period when she was married to French director Roger Vadim, creator of Brigitte Bardot's sex kitten period. Jane, and everyone else, called him simply "Vadim".

The year was 1965 and the film was "Cat Ballou", that wonderful western spoof. I'd taken Jane and Vadim to Berlin for the film's opening there. Back in Paris she was the guest of honor at a magnificent premiere. We held a party at the historic Mimi Pinson dance hall on the Champs Elysees and, because it happened to be Jane's birthday (her 28th, I believe), we had a special surprise gift for her.

I called Jane to the center of the empty dance floor. Hundreds of pairs of eyes were on her. The gift was brought in. It was a pony, a very nervous pony. As Jane took possession of the frightened animal it shat on the parquet floor, right on her shoes. She laughed nervously, not knowing what to do and not knowing if she really wanted a pony anyway.

I did the only thing I could do—called in the super pooper scooper brigade.

***

Erika Anderson is a beautiful actress and model with a wicked sense of humor and legs that go on forever. In 1990 she got her first big break with the title role of "Zandalee" for ITC. Her co-star was Nicolas Cage. At the time I worked at the Michael Dalling public relations agency and ITC was a client.

We managed to create a lot of interest in Erika among the independent distributors who would be releasing the film in Europe and I set up a promotional tour for her. She was to go to Italy, Spain, Holland, Belgium, England and Germany. I would accompany her and a girlfriend of hers. It was planned for late January, 1991.

On January 17, allied airplanes attacked Iraq and the Gulf War started. For several days we debated whether she would make the trip. I couldn't see that a war in far off Arabia would be a problem, but there was a lot of paranoia at the time and Erika, with pressure from her parents and friends, canceled.

The European distributors understood, with the exception of the Germans who took it as a personal affront.

The war was over in 43 days and by March we were ready to reschedule the trip. All the distributors were happy that it was on again—except the German. He told me on the phone that he wanted her only if she would appear nude on live television. He meant it. We didn't go to Germany.

We flew from Los Angeles to Rome, arriving exhausted several hours late and looking forward to a shower and a nap. It was not to be. The media were already assembled in the hotel for a press conference. Our carefully planned schedule had been changed because there was to be a newspaper strike the following day. A strike of some sort can virtually be guaranteed in Italy at any given time. Erika had 45 minutes to get ready. Gamely, she agreed to the change.

The following two days were set aside for magazine photo sessions. The magazines weren't on strike. After a good night's sleep Erika was ready for anything, including nude photo sessions. I discreetly left the room while the photos were being taken in a hotel room, but returned before they had finished, much to Erika's amusement.

We took a walk after lunch and, while waiting for traffic signals to change on a corner of the Via Veneto, Erika decided to give a busload of tourists a Roman thrill. As they drove by she lifted up her sweater and exposed all that she had.

The Spaniards are a more serious lot than the Italians and there were no requests for nude photo sessions in Madrid. The distributor's head of publicity was a sincere if somewhat uncool individual. He wore a dreadful wig and Erika dubbed him "rug-meister". On our second day in Madrid we declined his invitation to a heavy lunch and the three of us had sandwiches at a nearby fast food restaurant. As we were walking down Madrid's main shopping street on our way back to the hotel, Erika asked her friend to take a picture of her and me. We linked arms and grinned at the camera. Then Erika did her sweater thing again. I didn't see anything. I was grinning at the camera. But "rug-meister" did see. He happened to be crossing the street at the time and smiled with embarrassment. The incident nearly caused a traffic pile up. Erika just smiled. I never did see the photo.

Come to think of it, maybe we could have gone to Germany and done that nude television bit.

Erika had been particularly looking forward to Amsterdam. She knew that marijuana could be legally purchased at certain establishments and wanted to try it out. The first question she asked the local publicity woman was where could she buy a joint. The woman was disgusted. Apparently not all Dutch people had liberal ideas. At any rate, Erika and her friend had no trouble finding a café that could provide what she wanted. I declined her offer to join them. I just wanted to walk through the familiar streets and past the canals I had first visited when I was 13 years old.

I was getting dressed for dinner in my hotel room when I heard a knock. Opening the door, I found my way barred by dozens of plants which only moments before had lined the hotel corridor. I heard Erika giggling from behind her partially closed door. The next day there was another knock on my door. This time a banana and two oranges had been arranged in phallic splendor on the floor outside my room.

We drove from Amsterdam to the Hague, where we were entertained at a wonderful restaurant near the American embassy. On to Brussels, arriving at two in the morning. A few hours later we were up again, ready for a

OF KINGS AND QUEENS AND MOVIE STARS

screening of the film and a schedule of interviews in a distant suburb.

The drive back to Amsterdam that afternoon was a nightmare of detours and delays. We arrived late, ready for a few more interviews the next day. Then, on to London.

Two intense days of interviews were planned. Erika got through the first day, then that night became sick. We called a doctor who ordered her to stay in bed for 24 hours. The British publicist was angry, convinced that Erika was doing her Hollywood star bit. I couldn't convince him otherwise and, to this day, he does not believe her illness was genuine. He had to cancel 12 major interviews.

Erika and I remained friends. Back in Los Angeles, several months later, I was invited to a surprise birthday party for her. It was held at the Chateau Marmont, off Sunset Boulevard. Her friends had selected the very bungalow in which John Belushi had died. Most ghoulish!

***

DINNER WITH SIDNEY

During the sixties Sidney Poitier made a number of films for Columbia Pictures, including "The Long Ships," "To Sir With Love," "Guess Who's Coming to Dinner" and "Buck and the Preacher." The studio, however, did not always pay him a full salary but found other, more creative, ways of reimbursing him.

One year he was offered a vacation trip round the world with his four young daughters and their two governesses. I was asked to double as a travel agent and organized the European leg of his journey.

It so happens that I was taking my own summer vacation in the south of France while he was spending a few days at the Majestic Hotel in Cannes. I thought it would be a nice gesture to invite him and his family out to dinner one evening and he gladly accepted.

My only problem was that I had just loaned a famous, but temporarily embarrassed international celebrity most of my cash. Being a long way from home, I had no way to top up my wallet. As luck would have it, I couldn't use my credit cards, which were past their limits. I had recently paid them all off, but the checks had not yet cleared.

Earlier in the day my girlfriend and I drove in from the nearby resort town of St. Raphaël, where we were staying. We selected one of the finest restaurants in town and I had a long discussion with the owner, finally persuading him to forward the check to my Paris office where, I assured him, it would be taken care of.

We arrived promptly at the Majestic and told Sidney of my plans.

"Oh, no. I don't want to go there. I've been looking forward to taking my kids to La Colombe d'Or in St. Paul de Vence." I gulped. This was a very expensive restaurant in a beautiful medieval town in the hills 20 miles from Cannes. The check would probably be a king's ransom.

Before I could tell him that the restaurant would probably be full for such a large party, Sidney pre-empted me.

"I'll have the concierge book us a table," he said.

As I drove down the hotel's flower-lined driveway, followed by Sidney in his rented car, I wondered how the hell I was going to pay this bill. There were nine of us and the check would probably come to more than I made in a month.

We arrived at La Colombe d'Or and I ushered Sidney and his brood ahead of me. I shoved my business card into the maitre d's hand and, using my most authoritative voice, said, "Make sure our check is sent to my Paris office as soon as possible."

"Certainly sir," he replied obsequiously.

Phew, it had worked. Now I could really enjoy the meal.

And a wonderful meal it was. I diplomatically suggested that Sidney might want to select the wine. It was only for him and me. The rest of the party were into Cokes. He picked one of the most expensive bottles on the wine list. At this stage, that was fine with me.

"That wine was delicious wasn't it!" he said enthusiastically after we had emptied it. "Sixty three must have been a great year. Let's order another bottle."

I looked at him to make sure he was being serious. He was. "Sixty three is the wine's price, not its year," I explained gently. We ordered another bottle.

Back in Cannes later that evening, he invited me to join him and some friends he was meeting at a club. I happily accepted. The friends were Bill Cosby and Miles Davis. Although the evening was enjoyable I felt strangely out of place. When the three friends were together they fell into talking "jive" and it was almost like a foreign language to me. For the first time in my life I had a glimpse of what life must be like for blacks and other minorities in a white man's world.

***

IT'S A JUNGLE OUT THERE

One of the most extraordinary people I've met was neither an actor nor a filmmaker. She was a lady who lived in the middle of the African bush and became famous by writing a best selling book about a lioness she raised. Her name was Joy Adamson and the book was "Born Free."

Columbia Pictures produced a successful movie based on the book with Virginia McKenna portraying Joy Adamson. In 1966 the Austrian born author flew from her home on the Meru Game Reserve in Kenya to Vienna. I was waiting as the plane brought her back to her childhood home.

As we walked across the sterile concrete apron towards customs and immigration she stopped suddenly, bent down and picked something up off the ground.

At first I couldn't see what it was. Carefully she opened her hand and showed me a big, ugly, black bug.

"Es ist ein Mai-käfer," she said, explaining that it was a may bug. She told me that she felt sorry for the creature lost in a wilderness of cement. She would find a home for it once we got through customs.

When the customs officer asked us if we had anything to declare, Mrs. Adamson said, "only this," once again opening her hand. Before the man could say anything I explained that she had not really brought it into the country. Once outside the building, Mrs. Adamson carefully put down her new-found pet on a strip of lawn.

She was in town to give a series of press interviews and when we got in the car I showed her the schedule the local publicity manager and I had worked out. When I explained that the film had already opened, she asked to be driven straight to the theater. Even though she had just flown halfway round the world her hotel room and shower could wait.

So it was that we slipped quietly into the back of the cinema showing "Born Free" and watched the dramatic story unfold. Briefly, it tells of how she and her husband, George raised a lioness cub in their home and then released it back into the wild. The lioness, which they named Elsa, successfully survived in the bush yet would come back to visit, remaining uniquely both wild and tame. Tragically, Elsa was killed, not by other wild animals, but by poachers.

As the story unfolded on the screen Mrs. Adamson started crying. "My poor Elsa, my poor Elsa," she mumbled quietly. She had loved that noble creature so deeply that even seeing another lioness portraying Elsa had brought her to tears.

After a couple of days of interviews I took her back to the airport. The last image I have of her is her figure silhouetted against the open door of the airplane. Used to living in the bush, she couldn't bring herself to sit down in the air-conditioned plane until the last possible moment, when the door closed.

Joy Adamson and I corresponded for a few years after our Viennese encounter.

In one letter she wrote how she was now raising a family of cheetahs. I kept that letter. Here is an excerpt.

My cheetah family is getting rapidly wild now since the four cubs are able to move well—and well they do—some four to five miles within 24 hours. I still try to help feed them as it is a tough job for Pippa, their mother, to provide enough kills for these four hungry darlings. So I plod with a milk can with water, a basket full of meat, cine and still camera, a rifle, field glasses etc., often for many hours through thick bush, but often I have to return without having found a trace of these elusive creatures. I learned fascinating habits from these cubs, which are the first born wild to a man-reared mother. I feel extremely lucky to be allowed to share these precious cubs with Pippa—who is still as friendly as ever to ME, though now getting very selective with other humans.

Several years later Joy Adamson was herself shot to death by poachers. She had devoted her life to protecting wild animals only to be murdered by the wildest species of all. At last she was able to join her beloved Elsa.

***

FIRSTS

In the early 1980s I made my one and only trip to South America. Martin Ritt had directed the film "Back Roads" for CBS Theatrical Films. The star, Sally Field, had agreed to promote the movie in Argentina and I accompanied her on the long journey to Buenos Aires.

On trips of this nature it's standard procedure to offer a traveling celebrity two first class tickets and the Argentine distributor, who was footing the bill, naturally agreed to Sally's request to bring a friend along. Too late I learned that this friend was her personal publicist, Pat Kingsley.

Pat, a principal of the public relations firm PMK, is a publicist who approaches her work from a different direction than I do. I consider it my job to get as much strong, positive publicity for a film as I reasonably can. Pat believes in protecting her client. In fact, she is the leading Hollywood proponent of this "less is more" theory. Until recently she was Tom Cruise's publicist.

I was used to organizing trips of this nature directly with local publicists and presenting the touring star with an itinerary shortly before departure. In this instance I had to clear everything with Pat. As she was notorious for not returning phone calls, this became a problem. Nevertheless, I was gradually able to put the schedule together, explaining to Pat the importance and strategic value of each media interview.

It's a long way from Los Angeles to Buenos Aires. Somehow I didn't think you could fly for 16 hours and still remain in the Western hemisphere. We arrived exhausted, but forgot our fatigue with the warmth of our hosts' reception and the luxuriousness of our hotel.

We were soon in trouble, however. The name of a prominent columnist, writing for one of the city's major newspapers, had been inadvertently left off the schedule. Had I been there alone with Sally I would have slipped him into the timetable without a second thought and I'm sure there would have been no dissension from Sally.

Pat was less flexible. If the man was not on the original list he was not going to talk to her star. I thought this was a specious viewpoint and argued vehemently. Pat insisted that she'd done all the negotiating she was going to do on the already heavy itinerary back in Los Angeles. This writer was not going to talk to her client.

While our verbal battle was going on Sally sat quietly knitting in a corner of the hotel suite.

The banned writer had his revenge. Unable to interview Sally Field, he wrote a brilliant satirical piece about "the wardress" who protected the star from the marauding media. I thought it was hilarious. Besides, it mentioned both the film and the star and threw in a little harmless controversy; manna from a publicist's heaven.

A well-meaning local made the mistake of showing the piece to Pat Kingsley and the even greater mistake of translating it. Pat was livid with anger.

One morning before the interviews of the day started, I met with the Argentinean publicity chief for a cup of coffee at a nearby cafe. Suddenly, a green Falcon car came screeching to a halt outside the restaurant. Its four doors opened simultaneously and four men in leather jackets climbed out, slamming the doors behind them. I looked at my companion.

"If this were a movie they would be secret police," I said.

"This is no movie and they are," she replied.

The policemen moved from table to table demanding to see "papers." One man's credentials seemed to be suspicious and they were taken out to the car to be checked with headquarters.

It was a frightening moment. At this time the country was a dictatorship run by a cabal of corrupt generals. Thousands of innocent people, many of them children, had "disappeared" never to be heard from again. I knew this.

The man's papers were returned and the police left the cafe, having arrested no one. They had visited every table accept ours. I was vaguely disappointed. It would have made a better story.

My host explained that they hadn't spoken to us because I was obviously a foreigner and she was a woman. They'd been looking for a man.

Despite our disagreements, I got on well enough with Pat Kingsley and as our visit drew to a close, she and Sally told me that they were planning to spend a weekend's R&R in Rio de Janeiro on the way home. Would I like to join them?

I'd never been to Brazil and was delighted to accept, but thought I should check with my office first.

To my astonishment and great disappointment my boss told me, "the only reason they want you with them is so that you'll be there to pay all the bills. CBS is not going to cover the cost of their little vacation. I want you to fly straight back to Los Angeles. You'll have plenty of opportunities to visit Rio."

He was wrong. I still haven't seen Copacabana Beach.

***

CBS Theatrical Films also produced a wonderful tear-jerker titled "Table for Five" at about this time. Jon Voight portrays a father who decides to get to know his children by taking the three of them on a Mediterranean cruise. While on the ship he learns that his wife has died in a car crash and he has to break the news to the kids.

To promote the film in Tokyo I took Jon, the three child actors, their mothers and a tutor on a cruise to Japan, but we took the quick way—TWA.

It didn't take me long to find out that they do things differently in Japan. We were met by a small army of publicists, well, eight. These young people did the work of two in most other places. They were pleasant and seemed to be efficient, but I had no idea what most of them did. They were with us wherever we went around town, which meant that there were never less than 17 people in our group and frequently more, when senior executives from the distribution company, Nippon Herald, tagged along.

Personal appearance tours such as this can be tough on adults, but at times it must have been very difficult for the kids. Their tutor is also a state approved welfare worker. Her job was to give them three hours of schooling a day and to make sure they weren't used or abused. On one particular day we started at 10:00 a.m. and went through non-stop until 9:30 p.m., grabbing sandwiches on the way. Included in our day was a conference attended by 150 journalists and three TV shows in different

OF KINGS AND QUEENS AND MOVIE STARS   143

parts of town, two of them live, one by satellite to Australia. The children came through without a whimper.

Jon Voight seemed most at ease with the children. At other times he could be distant. One evening, our hosts invited us to a sushi restaurant. Jon said he would join us there later. While the rest of us were eating sushi and various Japanese delicacies, he was treating the kids to burgers at a nearby McDonalds, then on to a video arcade. He explained that he thought the children would enjoy a Big Mac more than a big raw fish. He was right, of course.

On the second day our group grew by one. A girlfriend of mine, a hostess with TWA, happily surprised me by rearranging her schedule and flying in from L.A. That evening, with the children in bed and Jon happily left to his own devices, we explored the town and managed to get thoroughly lost. Although the Japanese use the same Arabic numerals we do they don't bother to put them on street addresses so it was two in the morning before we found our hotel again.

I worked with Jon Voight again some 25 years later, part of the team handling the publicity on his film "September Dawn." Though Jon worked very hard publicizing the film, crisscrossing the country several times, it was a box office dud. There was one bright spot. I took him to the 2007 Montreal World Film Festival, where the film was screened and he was given a Lifetime Achievement Award.

***

NOW WE'RE COOKIN'

A major change in the way that Columbia Pictures distributed its films in the international marketplace occurred in the summer of 1971. The studio merged with Warner Bros for all their foreign releases.

Both studios had offices in almost every non-Communist country in the world. In Columbia's European office in Paris we supervised 19 countries, and that excluded the U.K. Now there could be only one office and one territorial manager in each country and that meant a tremendous upheaval for many loyal employees at both studios. The purpose of the change was, after all, cost cutting. Today it's called downsizing.

Senior executives huddled in New York dividing up the world like so many warlords. In Germany the Columbia manager got to stay, in other countries the Warner man got the job and the Columbia man got the ax. Their staff was also divided up and let go.

One of Columbia's most loyal managers was Rob Herzet in Holland, whom I have already mentioned in the "Lawrence of Arabia" story. Rob had worked for Columbia Pictures for 25 years. He was loyal almost to the point of boredom. Whenever I traveled to Amsterdam he would meet me at the airport and his sole topic of conversation was the business our films had done. Did he talk about politics? Did we discuss sports or the latest restaurant in town? Nah! So it was particularly painful when the Warner manager was chosen to run the new Dutch office.

Rob was a man loved by his staff and by the exhibitors he sold films to. I wish I could say the same about his replacement. The reason for the decision? Rob's health was delicate and he wasn't likely to be around much longer. The brass was right. Terribly hurt by the decision, his spirit broken, Rob died not long after being dismissed.

My own company loyalty had taken a beating and I no longer felt comfortable as a member of the "Columbia family."

Rumors started that Columbia's European office would be shifted to London, where Warners was based. My wife and I loved Paris and neither

OF KINGS AND QUEENS AND MOVIE STARS   145

of us was happy at the prospect of moving to London, even though I had family there. The rumors were confirmed. The big move would be in October. I began looking for alternative employment.

Jacqueline and I were good friends with director John Frankenheimer and his wife Evan Evans. John's passion was gourmet food and he was friends with many of the world's great chefs. He was a wonderful cook himself, so we particularly enjoyed our visits to their apartment on the Ile St. Louis, where he would prepare sumptuous meals.

John was aware of my wish to remain in Paris and began dropping hints that something might be available. For all my prodding, he refused to tell me what it was. This was a BIG SECRET, with delicate negotiations in the balance.

At this time Columbia was releasing Frankenheimer's "The Horsemen," starring Omar Sharif, and I traveled to Switzerland with John to do some press. It was here that I hit upon a devious plan.

After a dinner with the local Columbia representative, during which we enjoyed the usual libation, John and I returned to our hotel. I suggested a nightcap and brought a bottle of whisky to his suite. We talked of this and of that while I poured—two for him, one for me. He seemed unaware that I was nursing my drink while he was downing his.

It took the whole bottle, but eventually I sensed that he was relaxed enough. I brought up the subject of his big secret and out came the details of his ambitious plan.

For some time now he had been in discussion with France's top chefs and they had all tentatively agreed to prepare their most famous dishes for posterity and in front of video cameras. Frankenheimer would direct the initial videos himself, then leave it to someone else.

One must realize that this was 1971, when the video industry was in its infancy. Very few people had VCRs and the various "how to" video series we are all so familiar with, were many years in the future. John, in other words, was way ahead of his time.

He called his company "The Ten Greatest Cooks of France" and, in addition to the actual tapes, planned to market under the label kitchen equipment such as pots and pans and cutlery, sauces and wines. When this was up and running he was going to start a "Ten Greatest Cooks of Italy", then "Ten Greatest Cooks of Japan." Probably the only country that didn't lend itself to such culinary promotion was England.

It was a wonderful and daring idea, but what did this have to do with me?

"I want you to be president of the corporation," he told me, to my astonishment.

"I only want to be involved at the beginning, then I'll go back to making movies. I need you to run this on a full-time basis," he explained.

Apparently he was impressed by my marketing background and my interest in good food and good wine.

I was on cloud nine. I was going to be able to stay in my beloved Paris after all and would be working at something that was innovative and exciting with all the food I could eat.

I left his suite in the early hours feeling great—for about two seconds. I had been concentrating hard on remaining sober and alert during our conversation. Once outside, I relaxed and allowed the effects of the whisky to take hold. I was able to make my way back to my room only by holding on to the corridor walls. Fortunately nobody was around at that time of night.

"The Ten Greatest Cooks of France" never happened. Neither did their counterparts in Italy or Japan. Though the cooks themselves were happy to go along, their lawyers were not. They bickered among themselves over advertising billing, money and contracts to such a degree that the whole idea turned into a quagmire and had to be abandoned.

My wife and I didn't get to stay in Paris and in October we dutifully shipped our furniture and ourselves to London, back to the town where I had spent the first 30 years of my life.

It was good to be with my family again. My parents were still alive at that time and I had two brothers and their families living close by.

Since Jack Wiener had quit his position as head of European marketing to become a producer some three years earlier, his job had been split between Richard Dassonville, who handled advertising, and myself. Richard had confided to me that he was about to leave the company. I was well thought of at Columbia so I was a shoo-in to take over the department completely.

However, Jacqueline missed her Paris and didn't let me forget that for very long. When she became pregnant she intensified the propaganda. She wanted our baby born in France, not England. When she was six months pregnant with what we now knew were twins she went to Paris with my father to look for an apartment there. They found a beautiful place back in Meudon. It was a huge home at the crest of the Route des Gardes, the old road leading from Paris to Versailles. The building was nestled against the forest on one side and had a panoramic view of the city on the other side. How could I resist?

So I did the sensible thing. About to become a daddy twice over, I quit Columbia after nearly 11 years on the job, just as I was about to get the promotion I had been waiting for and crossed the channel to an uncertain future; no "Best Cooks," no film studio, just a few contacts and my own P.R. company. Three weeks after we had arrived in Paris our sons, Thierry and Benjamin, were born, two months premature.

***

I met up with John Frankenheimer again many years later, after I had moved to California and was working for CBS Theatrical Films. He had directed a film for the company titled "The Equals." starring Scott Glenn. This particular film had an awkward censorship problem in Taiwan. The Taiwanese don't particularly like the Japanese. So anything remotely Japanese was banned in Taiwan.

We had to persuade the Taiwanese authorities that this was not a Japanese film, even though it was made in Japan. I spent many hours at the Japanese consulate in Los Angeles obtaining the necessary documentary proof that all those actors with Japanese sounding names were, in fact, Americans who had required visas to work in Japan. Then it was on to the Taiwanese representative in L.A. to show him the proof.

Once we had that problem resolved, another one arose. The Taiwanese authorities didn't like our ending. It showed the Scott Glenn character breaking into the bad guys' headquarters and killing most everyone in sight. Fade out.

Revenge is sweet, but in Taiwan you cannot show crime going unpunished even if the good guy is doing it. The problem was solved by the local Taiwanese distributor. He shot a new ending at a cost of $50,000. A film crew was sent to the building in Kyoto, where the last scene had been shot. They hired a double for Scott Glenn and filmed a number of police cars racing up to the building, sirens blazing. Policemen got out and arrested Glenn. Justice had been served and the film could finally play in Taiwan.

Unfortunately, it didn't do any better there than it did in the rest of the world.

***

MUSIC TO MY EARS

My music tastes have evolved over the years and these days I keep pretty well to classical and jazz. Occasionally I'll get nostalgic and slip in a Beatles disc, an Edith Piaf or maybe a Herb Alpert.

But I don't know the first thing about music, couldn't tell a crescendo from a credenza. So it's strange that one day I was asked to fly 5,000 miles and make like an expert on the subject.

This was just a detour. I was making the trip anyway. I had received a phone call from British television who wanted to fly me from Los Angeles to London to appear as a guest on "This Is Your Life." The subject was Leslie Thomas, well-known English author, columnist and television personality. He and I had worked together as reporters on a local London newspaper when I was a 19 and he was 21.

I had just started working for Lorimar when the call came from Thames Television. My employers were happy to let me go and suggested that while in Europe I might want to "pop over" to Ireland to do a little business on their behalf.

The company was in production on the film "Avalanche Express" and had learned that they could get a great financial deal if they scored the music in Dublin. They wanted me to check out the studio and quality and availability of musicians.

My mouth dropped.

"I don't know anything about music," I protested.

"That's all right, we'll tell you what to ask and what to look for."

So it was that I sat down with Allyn Ferguson, the film's composer, who gave me a long list of technical questions I should ask as well as the make-up of the orchestra he wanted to hire.

"But I don't understand any of this."

"Don't worry. You'll fool 'em. Just take plenty of notes."

I had given them fair warning. If they weren't worried, why should I be?

My television appearance was most enjoyable. In addition to Leslie Thomas I met other old friends from my distant past.

I waited backstage as the program's popular host, Eamonn Andrews, gave his introductory spiel. He told Leslie:

"Back in 1952 you were a reporter on the Willesden Citizen. Each week it was someone else's turn to change the newspaper and photos in the paper's shop window. On this particular day you returned from lunch with a colleague and the two of you watched another reporter working in the window. Now this fellow's parents were from Holland and you had a special nickname for him. You called him "Moggy". This inspired you to burst into song thusly."

At this point we heard the slightly twisted words of a familiar song—"How Dutch is that Moggy in the window?"

That was my cue to walk on stage and be embraced by a surprised and delighted Leslie Thomas.

After the show, Leslie and I, plus a couple of old friends had dinner together. Coincidentally we were recognized by another colleague from our newspaper days. He came over to our table and apologized to me—for cold-cocking me during an argument we had had more than 20 years earlier. He had been a heavyweight semi-professional wrestler at the time. Apparently the incident had been playing on his conscience all these years. I smiled and we shook hands.

[A couple of years later I was again invited to appear on "This Is Your Life". I made the trip from Los Angeles to London to honor the well-known romantic novelist, television host and columnist Claire Rayner. In our teens and early twenties we had belonged to the same drama group and had played husband and wife in a play written by her then fiancé, Desmond Rayner. But this television appearance was not to be. Claire's brother, screenwriter/director Lionel Chetwynd, had developed an inner ear infection and was not allowed to fly. The show was rescheduled for six weeks later but that meant I would have missed my sons' birthday, so I refused to go despite the entreaties and blandishments of Thames Television.]

I left for Dublin the day after the Leslie Thomas show, my first trip to Ireland. It was not a happy experience. I managed to get food poisoning, so spent most of the time feeling very sorry for myself. Nevertheless, I was well enough to go to Ardmore Studios. You'd have thought that I owned Lorimar by the way they rolled out the red carpet. I knew I had to do all I could to play the role of a music expert magnificently and hide my ignorance. My host showed me the scoring stage where the orchestra would play while a large screen showed the scenes they would be accompanying. I nodded wisely as he pointed out its advantages. The control booth was even more bewildering, with arrays of boards loaded with buttons and dials and levers.

"We're very proud of this," he told me.

"And well you should be. Most impressive," I replied.

I asked questions I didn't understand and wrote down the incomprehensible replies. We talked about musicians, of trumpets and cellos, of first violins and second violins.

I murmured a few "ahas" and "mms" and once I even ventured to say "that's good, just what we need."

My host breathed a sigh of relief, shook my hand enthusiastically and would have kissed my ring and genuflected, had I allowed it, convinced as he was that I would authorize the music to be scored at Ardmore.

Back in L.A., I dutifully turned my notes over to Allyn. I believe the film's music was scored in California.

My personal experience with "Avalanche Express" was funny. I wish I could be equally light-hearted about the production. It was a tragic disaster. The director, Mark Robson died before the film was completed. When the producers and editors got a look at the footage he'd shot, it made very little sense. Robson was one of Hollywood's most successful directors, with films such as "Home of the Brave," "The Bridges at Toko-Ri," "Inn of the Sixth Happiness," "The Prize" and "Von Ryan's Express" in his résumé, so he hadn't been closely supervised. No one knew whether he had kept the final edit in his head or if his illness had affected his thinking and he really didn't know what he was doing. There were more holes in the film than in a lace doily.

Then, right at the end of the shoot, Robert Shaw, one of the stars, also died. I had worked previously with this brilliant actor on "A Man For All Seasons" and it was a sad loss indeed.

***

When I left Columbia Pictures in London in 1972 and established my own Paris based pan-European public relations company, my main client was National General Pictures, which went out of business some 18 months later. NGP was the distributor for First Artists, a company owned by Barbra Streisand, Paul Newman, Steve McQueen and other major stars. It was a concept based on United Artists, which had been formed by Douglas Fairbanks, Mary Pickford, Charlie Chaplin and D.W. Griffith.

One of the best films to come out of the First Artists stable was "The Life and Times of Judge Roy Bean" a western directed by John Huston and starring Huston, Paul Newman, Victoria Principal and Jacqueline Bissett (as Victoria's daughter, would you believe!). I think it's safe to say that this was the only film in which Paul Newman has sung to a bear.

The film was sold to independent distributors throughout Europe and we were all expecting good business. Then I started to hear rumors out of Italy, where musicals were considered the death of business. I heard that the local distributor was editing all the musical numbers out of the film, making it simply a straight western, instead of the idiosyncratic piece of whimsy that it was meant to be.

They denied that they had made any cuts, but aroused my suspicions when they told me it wasn't really necessary for me to attend a press screening they had planned in Milan. So I flew to Milan on November 28, 1972. I remember the date because it was my fortieth birthday and four days after the birth of my twin sons, Thierry and Benjamin. I think I could have flown to Italy without an airplane. Life literally begins at forty in my case.

So I was in a good mood when I walked, unannounced, into that screening room. It didn't even bother me very much to see that indeed all the music had been cut from the film. I returned to Paris and made my report. This time National General Pictures ordered the Italians directly to restore the film to its original concept.

They said they would. They didn't. "The Life and Times of Judge Roy Bean" did better in Italy, sans music, than in any other European country.

***

OF KINGS AND QUEENS AND MOVIE STARS

"Casino Royale" was a crazy James Bond parody released by Columbia Pictures in 1967. Everybody in the film was James Bond, including David Niven and Woody Allen. I was dispatched to Belgium to organize a fun-filled opening in Brussels. None of the cast was available so everything had to be home grown.

Belgium's most famous singer at that time was Adamo whom I engaged to star in a stage show before the film's premiere. As decorative background I hired 38 students at a local school for beauticians. I spent one day visiting the school and selecting my team of girls. I know—it's a hard job, but somebody had to do it! They were all dressed in figure hugging, show-stopping "Casino Royale" leotards.

A couple of days before the premiere I escorted five of the girls to the Brussels Motor Show for a little promotional goodwill. Dressed in their revealing leotards, they were a sensation. Mr. Lamborghini, designer of the sexy Italian sports car, was particular taken with them and dropped the promotion of his cars to talk at great length with my beauties.

In 2006 Sony Pictures released another version of "Casino Royale." There was only one James Bond this time.

***

While at the Moscow Film Festival one year, I was asked to be Sandra Dee's escort to a party. This star of all those "Tammy" movies and other light filmic desserts of the sixties, was both beautiful and pleasant, so this was hardly a chore. She was at that time married to popular singer Bobby Darren.

After dinner, the band began playing and, as any good escort should, I asked her to dance. She blushed.

"I know this sounds silly, but I don't know how to. Here am I, married to "Mr. Rhythm" and I can't even dance."

So we sat the evening out.

***

One of my favorite movies is "Cat Ballou". It also had one of the most memorable movie theme songs of all time, sung by Nat 'King' Cole and

Stubby Kaye. Cole, whose velvety voice was loved by fans all over the world, was known for singing in different languages, so we had the bright idea of asking him to cover "The Ballad of Cat Ballou" in French, German, Italian and Spanish. It would be a great promotion for those countries. The singer agreed to make the recordings.

Shortly afterwards, we received the tapes and Jack Wiener called me into his office to listen to them. I listened in horror. They were terrible. His voice was raspy and there was no vestige of that magic touch. His accent in the various languages was so bad that we couldn't understand what he was singing.

"What do you think?" asked Jack.

I shook my head in dismay. How could this be?

"They're terrible. I don't see how we can use them anywhere."

"You're right," he replied, sadly.

I looked at the tapes in my hand and, with a heavy heart, tossed them into a wastebasket.

A couple of days later we heard that "Nat 'King' Cole had died. I had thrown away the only copies of his very last recordings, an act that I've regretted ever since.

***

LEE MARVIN—AND OTHER BOOZERS

I've already mentioned "The Big Red One" and my adventures with the writer/director, Sam Fuller. Now I want to tell you about Lee Marvin, who starred in the picture as a tough infantry sergeant shepherding a platoon of G.I.s through the European front during World War II.

Lee's life off-screen was as rough and tough as his image on the screen. When I knew him he had quieted down, but he was the first to admit that in the not too distant past he had been a boozer and a brawler, ready to down a fifth or pick a fight with anyone who came along.

It was at this time that he was going through his highly publicized and precedent setting legal battle with Michelle Triola Marvin. During the court battle she claimed that she was destitute and, having been his companion for a number of years, she should be paid alimony now that they were separated. The word 'palimony' was coined in this lawsuit.

Marvin told me that he knew Michelle was living with Dick Van Dyke at this time and was, therefore, far from destitute. Unwilling to drag Van Dyke's name into this sordid battle, neither he nor his attorney mentioned him in court. They felt that they could win the case without it. They were right.

Strangely enough, several years later I was sitting by the pool at the Marina City Club in Marina Del Rey, California, when I became aware of a woman staring at me.

"Don't I know you?" she asked.

I don't believe so," I replied.

She introduced herself as Michelle Marvin. Lying in the chair next to her was Dick Van Dyke. I told her that I recognized her, but insisted that we had never met.

"In fact, I'm a friend of Lee," I said.

Her face brightened.

"How is Lee?" she asked. "Have you met his wife?"

"Yes."

"What's she like?"

"She's a very nice lady," I told her.

I saw Michelle and Dick frequently after that, during my weekend visits to the Marina City Club, where they lived at the time, but we never spoke of Lee again.

At the time of the release of "The Big Red One," in the early eighties, I arranged a trip to Amsterdam and London for Lee and his wife, Pam. I would be accompanying them.

Shortly before we left, Lee came to my office to discuss the press interview schedule that was being prepared.

"Before we go on this trip I want to promise you one thing," he told me.

"I'm sure you're concerned about my drinking. I want to assure you that's all behind me. I'm on the wagon now and you'll have no problems with me. Maybe I'll drink a beer or two, but that'll be it."

A strange confession for a star, but there was more to come.

We were met at Schiphol Airport, Amsterdam, by the distributor's effusive, if not obsequious, sales chief. He took us to the delightful Hotel de l'Europe, which sits on a canal across from the city's famous Mint Tower.

Lee was charming and uncomplaining through all the tedious questions put to him by the media over the next couple of days.

He bristled only on one subject—the aforementioned "Cat Ballou." In this film he portrayed the dual roles of a vicious killer and drunken ex-gunfighter, an acting juggling act that won him his only Academy Award as Best Actor. He told me that he hated the movie and his role in it. It was his least favorite part.

On our last night in town the distributor threw a dinner party at the de l'Europe for us and a few local theater owners. The sales chief could not do enough for us. He extolled the virtues of the very expensive wine he'd ordered.

When he offered Lee a glass, the actor demurred.

"But it is an excellent wine,"

"I don't drink."

"You must try it."

"No, thank you."

All this time I was frantically trying to signal the Dutchman to lay off Lee, to let it be. He didn't see me. He took Lee's refusal to drink as a personal affront. He pushed and pushed and finally Lee gave in. He drank a glass, then a couple more.

That was all it took. In surprising quick order he was drunk.

Fortunately, Lee didn't become aggressive. He didn't start a fight or burst into bawdy song. He simply became morose and morbid.

The dinner came to an end, we said our good-byes and Lee, Pam and I took the elevator to the fourth floor. At the door to his suite, Lee invited me in.

"We'll order a bottle of champagne from room service."

I pointed out that we'd be catching an early morning flight to London. We really needed to get to bed.

Now it was Lee who was insistent, so, unwillingly I agreed to stay for "just a glass."

Pam made her excuses and went to bed while Lee and I sat drinking until three a.m. The man obviously needed to talk. He told me about all his problems with drinking and revealed that his father had been an alcoholic too.

"He killed himself and it was all my fault, just as if I'd killed him with my own hands," he said.

Lee said that if he he'd treated his father right and listened to what he was trying to tell him, he could have saved his life.

"I killed him," he said again.

Feeling like an inefficient psychiatrist, I tried to persuade Lee that he couldn't blame himself for the action of others.

"We're all responsible for our own lives," I said.

Eventually Lee talked himself out and I left for my own room. I think he felt better for pouring his heart out.

We were both reasonably clear-headed the next morning and the London leg of the trip passed uneventfully.

A few weeks later Lee called me from his ranch outside Tucson, Arizona. He had obviously been drinking again and talked for 45 minutes.

He confessed that he'd made dozens of personal appearance tours in his career but he had never had so much fun as he had with me.

"I was able to relax with you," he said.

As a P.R. man this pleased me to hear since I thought a great deal of Lee, too. He was a great guy.

***

Talking of "Cat Ballou", that film came up many years later in one of the strangest film experiences I've had. It was the fall of 1997 and the movie was "Everything's George". One of the lead actors in the picture was dead and the director didn't—direct, that is.

The "George" of the title was George Burns, who had died a year and a half earlier, but we resurrected him through the magic of motion capture technology, the magnificent make-up of Academy Award winner, Kevin Haney and a terrific performance by Frank Gorshin "doing" Burns. Gorshin played another role in the film as well—an off-the-wall ex-FBI agent named Shelleen, named in honor of Lee Marvin's character in "Cat Ballou". The only problem with the film was the director, Scott Lane. He'd written a great script and should have left it at that. But he wanted to direct and star in the movie. He'd never directed before and probably never will again. He was also a lousy actor. As the pressure built up he turned to drugs, legal and prescription as well as booze and got into such a state that at one point he had to be escorted off his own stage. The director of photography was the real director of the film. Did I say Scott Lane was the only problem? There was another. Rodney Dangerfield was brought in for one day to play God. I think the part went to his head because he acted like he WAS God. He was supposed to be on the set for a full day, but upped and left after only four hours. No explanation. Now I knew why he didn't get any respect.

Some eight years later, when I was working for Murray Weissman, I came back from lunch one day and Murray told me we had a new client. It was a film called "Angels with Angles." He showed me the DVD he'd been given. As I looked at it I realized that this was "Everything's George," with a new title. Apparently Scott Lane had sobered up and had found the money to complete post-production on the film. He had come to our company purely by coincidence, but was delighted to learn that I was part of the team. Unfortunately critics panned the film.

***

Trevor Howard was another actor who liked his liquor. He came to Munich for several days in 1966 to promote a film whose title I have forgotten, and I don't think he had one sober moment.

On Trevor's first day in town, Columbia's manager in Germany, Erich Müller, took us to Rumpelmeiers, one of the most expensive and prestigious restaurants in all of Germany. Both Trevor and I ordered maatjes herring as hors d'oeuvre. As I bit into my first fork full I felt a sharp pain in my mouth. A sliver of glass was embedded there. I protested loudly.

Trevor mumbled in his slurred way, "I seem to be having the same problem, old boy," dreamily pulling several pieces of glass out of his mouth.

I was angry, Erich was aghast and Trevor just took it all in his stride.

The maitre d' came over, all a-tremble, explaining that nothing like this had ever, ever occurred before in his establishment. What could he possibly do to make amends?

"Just pay the hospital bill if we end up there," I said, suddenly magnanimous.

Trevor simply mumbled something about it being no problem at all.

I suppose in today's litigious world we would have threatened to sue the restaurant for a million DM., but those were kinder, gentler times.

The following day, Trevor failed to answer calls to his room. I found him lying in a drunken stupor and was unable to wake him. My only choice was to let him sleep it off and re-arrange his schedule.

He came to in the evening and insisted on meeting me at a nightclub he had heard about.

"Are you sure you want to do this?" I asked, quite sure I did not want to do this.

"Absolutely, I'll be fine. It's supposed to be a great place. Lots of beautiful girls."

Grudgingly, I agreed to meet him there and besides, he was right about the girls.

We spent the evening together. He didn't do much drinking, but then, like Lee Marvin was to show several years later, he didn't need much to get drunk.

In my mind, I can still see Trevor Howard dancing all alone on an empty floor, holding an imaginary partner in his arms.

***

I am not particularly proud of this next episode and, as with many unpleasant incidents, I've managed to forget much of what happened.

George Peppard was in Paris to promote "The Victors" and I took him to Jimmy's, the 'in' night spot, for an informal interview with a writer from Paris Match. We were all drinking pretty heavily and I lost my usual polite reticence. Peppard was being the obnoxious Hollywood star, rude and demanding.

"You can go to hell," I slurred and, turning to the reporter, I continued, "See, that's the way we talk to our stars at Columbia Pictures."

I was very fortunate. Either George and the reporter were as drunk as I was or they just didn't care. My insult passed without comment or repercussions.

Later on that evening, the club's owner, Regine, who was the queen of Paris night-life, invited us to her apartment for a spaghetti dinner that she prepared herself. All was well after all. In the strange hierarchy of Paris society, this was the most sought after invitation you could get.

***

More recently, in the fall of 1994, I was unit publicist on the film "Leaving Las Vegas," written and directed by Mike Figgis and starring Nicolas Cage and Elisabeth Shue. Nick is not a boozer to my knowledge but he played one in this picture. His character was drunk, or pretty close to it, throughout the movie. He portrayed a screenwriter who goes to Las Vegas to drink himself to death. Just to make sure he got it right the producers hired a "drinking coach" named Tony Dingman. Tony showed the star how to walk, talk, fall and get up and fall again. One day, during the first week of filming, we were in Laughlin, Nevada. Tony persuaded Nick that the only way he could get the right feel for the scene was to get blitzed himself. Well, Cage drank non-stop, in his room, in the hotel bar, wherever he could get his glass filled. By the time he was ready for his big scene he was almost out of it. During the shot he knocked a waitress to the ground. He was supposed to do that. He also managed to knock over and destroy a blackjack table and cut his hand in the process. He was not supposed to do that. He never touched a drop after that night. He told me that he wanted to try it for real just the one time. After that he went back to acting a drunk.

Tony complained to me later that Nick wouldn't drink anymore. "How does he expect to get it right?" he asked. Of course Tony was a confessed alcoholic. I never saw him unconscious but he never looked totally sober either.

The script was based on a semi-autobiographical book by John O'Brien who blew his brains out two weeks after signing the contract for the movie. A touching moment came when his entire family visited the Los Angeles set. They were deeply moved by the filming and the attention they got from the stars and crew. They also saw an amazing physical resemblance between Nick and John. The father felt that the movie was a fitting tribute to his son and they all went back to their home in Cleveland happy at this immortalization.

"Leaving Las Vegas" was one of the most critically acclaimed films of 1995. At the 1996 Oscar® ceremonies Cage won the Academy Award® for Best Actor in a leading role having previously won the Golden Globe® as Best Actor in a Dramatic Film. The film was nominated for three other Oscars®—Best Actress for Elisabeth Shue, Best Director and screenplay based on material previously produced or published, both for Mike Figgis. The $3,500,000 film, shot in 16mm, won four Independent Spirit Awards—Best Film, Best Director, Best Actress and Best Cinematography.

***

STEVE McQUEEN

When we're all gone and Hollywood is just part of this planet's cultural heritage, historians might amuse themselves by putting together a list of disagreeable stars from the past. If they did so, Steve McQueen would be right up there close to the top. McQueen was really more than disagreeable. He was nuts!

I first met him at Orly Airport in Paris in 1973 when he was ostensibly arriving to promote "The Getaway" together with his co-star on and off screen, Ali MacGraw. I use the word "ostensibly" because when I approached him he brushed me aside.

"I'll find my own way to my hotel, and don't you follow me," he admonished.

I was in a difficult position here. I indirectly represented the producers, First Artists (through the distributors, National General Pictures) and he was one of the partners in the company. NGP had paid for their trip and was expecting me to set up some major media interviews. He and I had to talk.

I did as he asked. I didn't follow him. I was waiting at the private hotel on the ritzy Avenue Foch when he arrived.

"What the hell are you doing here and how did you find out where I was staying? My hotel was supposed to be a secret."

I explained that New York had told me where he would be staying because they wanted me to set up interviews.

"I won't do any interviews," he said, walking over to the reception desk before I could respond. He checked in, leaving me nonplused.

From the other side of the lobby he beckoned me imperiously. I hate it when that happens. I've always believed that if you want to talk to someone you go to them, no matter how important you think you are. But then I always return phone calls too, so that makes me very un-Hollywood.

Nevertheless, I accepted his summons and crossed the lobby.

It seemed he had changed his mind.

OF KINGS AND QUEENS AND MOVIE STARS 163

"If we're going to work together you will never wear that coat in my presence again. You will take it home and burn it. You should wear a leather jacket and turtleneck sweaters. Do I make myself clear?"

I nodded because there was really nothing to say under this bombastic assault. I rather liked my long lambs wool coat, but if it meant we could get some interviews in I'd happily leave it at home.

This man had more twists and turns than a mountain road.

All this time Ali had said nothing, but smiled sympathetically at me. I had the feeling that she was used to this kind of verbal assault.

Again I brought up the subject of press interviews.

"I will do one interview only," he said.

"But...," I began.

"One interview! And if there's any argument I won't do that."

I quickly made a silent run through of the possible press. If there was going to be just one shot I wanted it to be Paris Match, the top selling weekly magazine. I might even be able to get a cover.

To my relief, McQueen agreed to do the photo shoot.

"But it will have to be at Le Mans in two days. I'm taking Ali there to show her where I made the movie ["Le Mans"]." He gave me the name of the hotel where they would be staying, vowing me to silence.

The hotel doorman interrupted to tell McQueen that the self-drive Mercedes he had rented was waiting outside. A photographer was also waiting.

Steve's fury erupted again.

"How the hell did he find out I was here?"

He looked at me accusingly. I shrugged my shoulders. He had probably been tipped off by one of the hotel staff.

"I'll take care of him," McQueen said, stalking out of the hotel followed by Ali and myself.

The waiting photographer raised his camera and Steve brushed him aside.

"I'll smash your damn camera in your face if you try to take a picture," he said.

"Come on, Ali. Get in the car," he said, gunning the engine.

The valiant cameraman again tried to get in his exclusive shot. Steve drove the Mercedes right at him. The photographer leapt out of the way, but didn't quite make it. He was hit by the right fender and thrown to the ground.

Steve screeched to a halt twenty yards away, then reversed the car to where the photographer was unsteadily getting to his feet.

He climbed out of the car, apparently realizing that he'd gone too far.

"Are you all right?" he asked.

The man felt himself all over, stretched his bruised body and looked at his miraculously undamaged camera.

"I think so." Then, sensing that the actor might be more amenable after the accident, he asked if he could get just one shot.

This started McQueen up all over again. He began screaming at the photographer.

Right here I lost my own patience.

"Steve, get in the fucking car and get out of here. Don't make matters worse. I'll take care of the photographer. That's my job. Now go!"

McQueen's mouth dropped open. He started to stay something, then changed his mind. Without another word he drove off, going west and out of town. I don't think he was used to anybody talking to him that way.

The photographer ran for his own car, planning to follow him. Persistent paparazzo! I grabbed his arm.

"Now why don't we just wait here a little while and chat," I said amiably.

Back in my office, I called Paris Match and let them sell me on an exclusive story. I agreed, only on the condition that I get a cover. That was as good as it got for a publicist in France at that time. I hooked up with the photographer and we agreed to take the train the 200 kilometers to Le Mans.

I spoke to my boss in New York and explained what had happened. He was sympathetic, knowing McQueen's reputation, and told me not to worry about doing any more than the Paris Match gig.

Two days later the photographer and I arrived at McQueen's hotel in Le Mans. Ali MacGraw was the first downstairs. She looked pale and stressed out. I took her to one side and asked if everything was okay.

"Leonard, I think what Steve told you about your coat and telling you to burn it was terrible, but don't feel too badly. He did the same thing to me today."

I looked at her, puzzled.

She continued, "We had a huge row this morning and he blamed it on my top coat. He said that every time I wore it we fought. So he picked up the coat and threw it in the trash. There's going to be one happy chambermaid here today. That coat cost me $300."

Ali started to walk away, then turned back and said quietly, "You probably wonder why I stay with this man."

"The thought had crossed my mind."

"I stay because I love him. I know what he is, but I can't help myself."

Ali MacGraw was as sweet as McQueen was mean. It was a strange match.

In due course, Steve joined us downstairs, surprisingly affable. We drove over to the nearby race-track for the photo shoot.

As the photographer made preparations Steve said casually, "By the way, I will only let you shoot in black and white."

"But why?"

"Because that is what I want."

I told Steve that the Paris Match covers were always in color. We were going to blow the whole deal. And what difference did it make to him whether the pictures were in color or black and white?

"Take it or leave it. Black and white."

The photographer shrugged. He wasn't about to get into an argument. He was getting paid either way. He popped a roll of black and white film into his camera and took a series of shots of Steve and Ali happily leaning against a guard-rail.

Paris Match used the photo in the following week's issue. It was deep inside, single column, two inches—and black and white.

I don't know what the trip had cost National General, but I don't think it was a very good investment.

I, however, did make a good investment. I followed Steve McQueen's advice and bought a leather jacket and a bunch of turtleneck sweaters.

Several months later I happened to be in Munich when I received a call from a journalist from Bild Zeitung, Germany's highest circulation newspaper.

It was true, wasn't it, that I was a very close friend of Steve McQueen and

Ali MacGraw, the reporter insisted.

"Why do you ask?" I said.

"Well, we have it on good authority that a few days ago they got married on a Caribbean island and you, as one of his best friends, were an official witness."

"No comment," I replied.

Steve and Ali had indeed tied the knot a few days before, but I wasn't there and didn't find out about it until several days later.

***

DISASTERS AT DEAUVILLE AND MONACO

Shortly after Universal Studios elevated me to the exalted title of "Executive Director of International Advertising and Publicity", I went to Deauville to represent the company at this delightful Normandy film festival, which I had missed out on a few years earlier when William Friedkin made his last minute cancellation.

I call it delightful because it has none of the tension, egomania and general money driven madness of its sister event held every spring in Cannes. (Perhaps I would have had a different perspective if I had been there with Friedkin!)

Business is discussed on the tennis courts and over lunches in wonderful restaurants. The evenings are given over to cocktail parties, dinners and, of course, the screening of films, which is what this is all about. This is a festival of only American movies and all the major studios are well represented.

Outside the United States, Universal's film distribution and marketing was handled by a London based company, United International Pictures. Universal was part owner of UIP together with Paramount and, at the time, MGM/UA, whose films were also distributed by this organization.

UIP was headed at this time by Michael Williams-Jones, a typically reserved Englishman who probably had more clout in the international film market than anyone else. As the chief of advertising and publicity for one of his parent companies I had a very delicate balancing role to play. I realized that he and his marketing team in London resented any interference on my part because they knew what they were doing and were doing it well. On the other hand, I owed it to Universal and to the studio's producers to make sure OUR films did not get lost in the crush of films from Paramount and MGM. That was, in fact, my mandate when I had been given the job.

I gave no instructions, merely made suggestions. They pretended to appreciate my ideas. I pretended not to be irked by the constraints.

After Deauville I was planning to fly to London for meetings at UIP headquarters before traveling on to Los Angeles. This is a complicated journey, involving taking a train the 200 kilometers to Paris, a taxi from the Gare du Nord to the Charles De Gaulle Airport, a flight to London, then a taxi from Heathrow to my hotel in Piccadilly. Haughty in my new title, I had UIP charter a plane instead, which would make the short hop over the English Channel from Deauville directly to the U.K.

At the time of departure the skies turned black and the wind howled. A major storm had appeared from nowhere and was churning up white caps in the Channel. I thought twice about taking the plane but I'd used my new power and had put them to a lot of trouble. So, I sold myself a bill of goods. After all, how bad could it be? The flight wasn't more than half an hour anyway.

Michael Williams-Jones, so staid, so proper, so utterly British, dressed magnificently as always, joined me on the short flight, together with some other executives.

After the plane lifted off from Deauville and headed for those ominous clouds, I began to regret my action. Michael, sitting next to me, chatted amiably with the executive across the aisle. Neither seemed to care that we were being tossed around like a shuttlecock in a badminton tournament. I clung to the seat in front of me, my knuckles the proverbial white. The rest of me was turning the equally proverbial green.

I looked for the brown paper bag that I had always seen in front of airline seats but had never used. Wouldn't you know it? You can never find a paper bag when you need one.

I turned to Michael to ask if he could find a bag, as he had the aisle seat. I never got the words out. Instead, I threw up all over his beautiful navy blue blazer and well-polished black brogues. A look of horror etched itself into his face. I had never felt so miserable in my life.

I apologized, of course, but there was nothing I could say to make up for the foul smelling catastrophe I had created.

When I showed up at the UIP office in Hammersmith the next morning, the entire staff, from the doorman on up, knew what I'd done. I had to endure jokes from everyone—except Michael, who I don't think ever forgave me. Well, maybe he did. I bumped into him again about eight years later. He was friendly enough, but he did make a point of reminding me of my moment of infamy.

OF KINGS AND QUEENS AND MOVIE STARS 169

***

In November of that same year I planned a seminar for the managers and publicity directors of UIP's major territories. The man at Universal who had promoted me, Charles Glenn, had suggested Monte Carlo as the site and I certainly could not fault him on his taste.

Michael Williams-Jones and his senior marketing executives would also be attending and I booked us all into the Hotel de Paris. I arrived ahead of time to go through plans with our French publicity people, who were doing the ground work.

Charles Glenn was due to arrive the next day with an assistant and the slides and carousel for his audio-visual presentation. We got word that his flight had been delayed several hours. He had to be exhausted. I made the decision to send "Mr. Fix-It" to Nice Airport to meet him. He was a man out of UIP's Paris office who had been known to work miracles with officials. If anyone could get Charles and his material through customs and immigration in a hurry he could. Even Lew Wasserman, chairman of MCA, Universal's parent company, used him for delicate errands.

I had finished a working lunch at the hotel when I called the front desk to see if Charles had arrived. Yes, he was on his way up to his room. I prided myself on my timing, waited a couple of minutes, then called up to his room.

"Hi, welcome to Monte Carlo," I said brightly. "I'd like to have a word with you, if you have a moment."

"Yes, I want a word with you too. Get up here right now."

"You weren't at the airport to meet me," he said unhappily as I walked into his suite.

"No, I was in a meeting and I sent the person best equipped to handle things at the airport to prevent any further delay or inconvenience to you. What's the problem?"

Only one. You weren't there. I hired you. You work for me and when I arrive at an airport or anywhere else you will be there waiting for me. I've a good mind to throw you out of that window right now!"

"But that's eight floors down," I replied respectfully.

As he continued, he ripped open a small envelope that came with a bottle of Dom Perignon champagne sitting on a table.

"I demand that you show me the respect I deserve," he said.

I was feeling wonderful as he read the note. I knew what it said because I had sent the champagne— "Welcome to Monte Carlo. I hope you have a wonderful time here."

Apart from this opening scene, the meetings went well. On our last evening in Monte Carlo we organized a farewell dinner. Because November is the "off" month in the Midi, the out-of-town restaurant was specially re-opened for our party.

A fleet of cars drove us through twisting roads to our destination, a quaint old place, nestled in the hills several miles from Monaco. By the time we arrived I started to feel unwell and as I sat down I realized I would not be able to eat a thing. I made my excuses, said my good-byes and took one of the cars back to town.

The closer we got to Monte Carlo, the better I began to feel and by the time we arrived back at the Hotel de Paris all trace of sickness had gone. I ordered a sandwich in my room. Now what was I to do? I certainly didn't feel like going to bed. I decided that a few hands of blackjack at the casino next door would be just what the doctor ordered.

I sat down at the blackjack table and won the first hand, and the next, and the following hands. It was amazing. I couldn't lose. I looked at my watch anxiously. My colleagues could be returning at any minute. This being our last night they would probably be hitting the tables too. It would be awkward if they found me here when I was supposed to be sick in bed. I decided to quit after I lost just one hand. That took quite a while, but finally I did lose—to my relief.

I got back to the hotel without seeing anyone and left early in the morning for the airport. It was only several days later that I learned the entire group had gone to Loews Casino on the other side of town. I could have stayed all night and wouldn't have been disturbed. I would also have doubtless lost my shirt.

When I returned to Los Angeles, I heard from a colleague that Charles had seriously wanted to fire me for my "outrageous" behavior, but had been talked out of it. My unfortunate accident over the English Channel didn't impress him too much either.

He had also tried to fire my predecessor at Universal, Nadia Bronson, but had failed. Nadia had been an assistant to a man who had held the job for some 40 years. When he was diagnosed with cancer she filled in and her temporary position drifted into a permanent one. Charles was not happy with her work, but by the time he made up his mind to dump her she was pregnant and firing her would have been illegal. So he decided to keep her on and bring me in over her in a totally new position. He didn't want to tell her while she was carrying her baby and waited until after the birth. She was called in, thinking that Charles only wanted to see her new baby. Was she in for a surprise! Nadia went ballistic, accusing me of plotting against her, which was untrue.

Her initial reaction was to quit and I moved into the beautiful corner suite she had occupied at Universal Studios. She stayed away for the full six weeks of her maternity leave then, with 24 hours to go, she changed her mind and returned. She had hired Gloria Allred, a high profile attorney who manages to get her face on television and in newspapers with astonishing frequency. She threatened to sue Universal Studios and Lew Wasserman for sexism even though she had been neither fired nor demoted. If she had been a man she would have been fired outright. So much for sexism.

Nadia was given another office, almost as big as mine. This didn't seem to bother her. She made the greatest fuss about her parking spot. She determined not to lose it. That didn't bother me. I was more interested in where I parked my buns than my car.

We had an uneasy truce. I let her get on with her work, which was mainly the servicing of material to the various branch offices round the world. I concentrated on relations with producers and with UIP, coming up with creative ideas and traveling when necessary.

This didn't last very long. Bob Rehme, head of the motion picture division, was ousted and new management took over. Charles Glenn was the next to go. Following Charles' threats to fire me it was ironic that he should be fired first.

He was succeeded by Marvin Antonowski, a dour man who hardly seemed aware of his own executive staff. If he recognized you at all it would be with a barely perceptible flick of his wrist as he walked by.

On one occasion, after he'd been there about a month, I entered into his sanctum and asked him to greet two important visiting foreign journalists. He nodded his agreement, stepped outside and, with a big grin pasted uncomfortably on his face, extended his hand to the first person he saw.

"Hello, I'm Marvin Antonowski," he said, pumping the man's hand.

Unfortunately, the man was Fred Skidmore, who worked in the very next office to Antonowski, and not a visiting journalist.

Marvin started bringing his own people in. One of them, Ed Roginski, was a friend of Nadia's, unfortunately for me. She called him on a regular basis at Columbia Pictures where he still worked, asking him to make sure she got control of the department again. She told him that she couldn't wait for things to be the way they were before I arrived. Friends of mine warned me about these calls but I didn't see there was much I could do.

Sure enough, Roginski, who took the number two position in the department, arrived on a Wednesday. I met him once when he toured the department. Two days later I was called into his office and fired. I was told there was no place for me in the new structure. The day was known as Black Friday because almost every department head in the marketing division was fired that day, including my old friend Fred Skidmore. On his arrival at Universal, Antonowski had gathered his entire staff together and had promised there would be no firings under the new regime.

Nadia left Universal 17 years later with the title of President of International Distribution and Marketing. I hold no grudge. Life's too short.

A year after I left the studio Ed Roginski died of complications from AIDS. Antonowski was out not much later. My assistant at Universal, a wonderful man named Paul Lindenschmidt, also died of AIDS at about the same time. My secretary, Susanne, whom I had inherited from Alfred Hitchcock, died of cancer a day after Paul passed away.

Charles Glenn is today a good friend. After all, it's only business.

***

COLD BLOOD

When Random House published Truman Capote's "In Cold Blood" in 1965 it became a sensational best seller. This was the first of a whole new genre of literature, a work of non-fiction that read like fiction.

The film was released by Columbia Pictures some three years later, with Richard Brooks directing.

Brooks, Truman Capote and one of the stars, Robert Blake traveled to Munich and Amsterdam in the early spring of 1968 to help launch the film in West Germany and the Netherlands. Blake was a dour, miserable and uncooperative fellow. [Thirty-three years later his still unpleasant personality would be aired before the entire country after his wife had been murdered.]

The difference between Richard and Truman was striking. You could not imagine two more different men, yet they were the best of friends.

Richard Brooks was a quiet, pipe smoking, very masculine guy, while Truman was this fey little creature with his familiar squeaky voice, head too big for his body and exaggerated, effeminate gestures. He gave an impression of total helplessness.

I had this urge to put my arms around his shoulders and say, "there, there, little boy, everything's going to be all right."

Then I would remember the book and the movie and think of the mind that created them. Capote was no helpless child, but one tough cookie with a razor sharp mind. If you could get past his outlandish image you could understand the friendship between these two men.

In Amsterdam we stayed at the Hilton Hotel, located in the southern suburbs. After a press lunch at the downtown Hotel de l'Europe, Richard Brooks suggested that we walk back to our hotel.

"That's a helluva long way," I told him.

"Come on, what are you, a wimp?" he taunted. "How far can it be?"

"Far," I replied laconically. "But if you're game, so am I."

So we set out. The weather was fine and I love the sights and sounds and smells of Amsterdam anyway.

We walked and we walked. Our pace began to slow. We walked some more.

"How much farther?" Richard asked, obviously unwilling to admit that he was tiring.

"Oh, we're about halfway," I replied.

He grinned.

"I guess you were right. Let's get a cab."

That evening Truman Capote and I were sitting alone in the bar of the Hilton Hotel. He was very upset. He had lost his valuable address book, filled with the names, phone numbers and addresses of his elite circle of friends. Whoever had found—or stolen—it must have had a field day. The address book was never recovered.

He was a charming, vulnerable fellow, I thought as I looked at him over the rim of my glass of genever. Yet it was he who had written "In Cold Blood" which is the story of the brutal murder of a family of four by Dick Hickcock and Perry Smith and of their ensuing trial and execution. The killing was the subject of sensational headlines across the country, not only because of its unprecedented violence, but because it occurred in a quiet rural community in western Kansas.

Capote found a strange fascination in this macabre case and became involved even while the investigation was still going on. He wanted to get deep into the minds of these killers, to try to understand and convey to his readers what kind of men could commit such an act and why they would do it. He not only succeeded in his task but also became friends with the two killers, frequently meeting with them in their prison cells.

After a few drinks, Capote relaxed and his mood changed. It was obvious that he wanted to get something out in the open.

"I am going to confess something to you that I never had the courage to put into "In Cold Blood" and it is something I have never told anyone else," he said.

"Perry was sentenced to die by hanging and I was asked by the authorities to be an official witness. It wasn't something I wanted to do. The idea of it terrified me, but being so close to him all this time I felt I owed it to him.

"The execution was to take place in a big old red barn. The gallows was set up at one end. I lost myself in the crowd of people at the other end.

OF KINGS AND QUEENS AND MOVIE STARS

There came the time when they led Perry up the wooden steps to where the rope was waiting for him. He was asked if he had any last request before he died. 'Yes,' he said. 'I want to say something to Mr. Capote.'

"They called my name and asked me to come forward. I wished the ground would open up and swallow me. I would rather have been anywhere on the earth's surface than in that terrible place. Again they called my name, more impatiently this time.

"I had never known anything to take as long as that walk. My legs were trembling as I climbed the five steps up to the gallows where Perry stood, the rope just inches from his head and mine.

"Perry moved towards me. I tried not to flinch. He bent down and whispered in my ear, 'Tru, I love you. I've always loved you.' Then he kissed me. Those were the last words he ever spoke.

"I started crying as I made my way back across the barn floor. I desperately wanted to be anonymous, to be lost in the crowd again. I cried as they adjusted the rope around his neck and his body dropped through the trapdoor. I cried in the train all the way home. I cried for three days."

In a way I understand Perry's last words. The book had explored his soul and had tried to make some sense out of the senseless killings. Truman had done this for him and helped him put his house in order. Capote was indeed a great and sensitive man.

"In Cold Blood" was a book that had a tremendous impact on the public's attitude towards capital punishment. Richard Brooks created a masterpiece in his definitive film version and it was as successful and controversial as the book.

[In 2005 much of what I had been told by Tru was captured in the film "Capote."]

ODDS AND END

Quote # 1: Rosalind Russell, in London for the opening of "Five Finger Exercise" in 1962 after I'd displeased her for some reason which I no longer recall.

"Nobody talks to Roz Russell like that. Nobody! I am an institution in this industry."

I refrained from making the obvious comment that an institution was where she belonged. It was too easy. And it would have got me fired.

Quote # 2: Joseph Heller, author of the best selling book "Catch 22", was sitting in my London office at the time of the film's release when he received a call from Lord Bertrand Russell, inviting him to spend a week in his lordship's castle in Wales. Lord Russell was a Nobel laureate and Britain's foremost philosopher.

"How about that! Little Joe Heller from Coney Island going to spend a weekend in a castle with a lord."

The phone rang again a few moments later. Heller piped up:

"If that's the prime minister tell him I'm busy!"

Quote # 3: "The Collector" was a bizarre film about a butterfly collector (Terence Stamp) who also collected a girl (Samantha Eggar) and kept her a prisoner in his home as if she herself were a rare butterfly. When I asked the writer John Fowles, on whose book the screenplay was based, where he got the idea, he looked at me in mild surprise and said, "Well, that's my fantasy. Isn't it every man's?"

Quote # 4: Shortly after I moved to Paris in 1963 I answered the phone in my office. A man with a high-pitched querulous voice and a thick, mittel European accent was on the other end.

"I want to speak to the head of publicity," he said.

"I'm his assistant. Can I help you?"

"Yes, you can. This is Samuel Goldwyn and I want to know what it is you are doing with my "Porgy and Bess" in Paris. It should be released years ago. Why do you not open it?" he demanded.

Embarrassed, I explained that we were waiting for just the right theater. "West Side Story" had been running for four years at the George V Cinema and that was obviously the home for his "Porgy and Bess". We were waiting for "West Side Story" to finish its run so that "Porgy and Bess" could have the same success. He was only partly mollified.

Poor man! When we did eventually open his picture at the George V it ran for four weeks, not four years. I guess the French weren't ready for a musical about blacks.

***

Anthony Mann was one of Hollywood's most respected directors. He had helmed such films as "The Heroes of Telemark," "The Fall of the Roman Empire," "El Cid," "Cimarron," "God's Little Acre," "The Man from Laramie," "The Glenn Miller Story," "Winchester 73" and many more. He was also a man with a quick and violent temper.

In 1967 I was sent from Paris to Berlin where Mann was shooting "A Dandy in Aspic," starring Laurence Harvey, Mia Farrow and Tom Courtenay. I'd brought several journalists to the set and they had successfully done their interviews. Shortly before I left the location for Tempelhof Airport Mann called me over. He was furious that his day had been interrupted by the press visit. The fact that he had agreed to the junket had no bearing. The more he shouted, the angrier he became. He screamed at me for a long time, his face red and his veins almost bursting from his head.

An hour later, while I sat in the plane on my way back to Paris, Anthony Mann was having a massive heart attack in Berlin. He dropped dead in the middle of rehearsing a scene. I learned of the tragedy when I returned to my office and it was a long time before I overcame my guilt for having, perhaps, caused his death.

The executives at Columbia Pictures asked Laurence Harvey to take over as director for the remainder of the shoot. This was not, however, the only out-of-the ordinary responsibility given to Harvey. Mia Farrow was at this time engaged to Frank Sinatra, an old friend of Laurence. The singer asked his friend to look out for Mia, to be a sort of Dutch uncle for her.

While I was still in Berlin and before I had my heavy-duty session with Anthony Mann, I found out how hard a task this could be. Tom Courtenay took me to one side, seeking advice. The 30-year-old actor, his Yorkshire accent still thick, had a problem.

"Mia wants to have sexual intercourse with me and I don't know what to do about it," he told me. "What should I do?"

I would never have messed with the chairman of the board's girl friend in a million years. Sinatra had connections in all the wrong places. I told Tom this.

"Back off," I advised him.

"But she does want to do it and she is very beautiful," he said wistfully.

"Well, then you'll just have to make your own mind up," I replied.

He nodded. I never did find out if the two of them consummated their friendship.

***

Bertrand Tavernier is today one of France's most respected film directors, but when I first knew him he was a part-time, poorly paid publicist.

He worked for Columbia Pictures from time to time, representing the occasional French film we became involved with. Even back then, in the early sixties, he was passionate about films. He saw every film he possibly could.

It was part of my job at Columbia Pictures to organize private screenings for various purposes—for the media, for theater owners, for opinion maker groups and, if I wished, for my friends. That was one of the better perks. Somehow, as if he had his own private antenna out there, Bertrand always found out about these screenings. He would show up at the door to the screening room, lean and lanky, and always dressed in the same shabby raincoat, begging to be allowed in. Usually, if it was not a VERY private showing, I would let him through.

We stayed in touch over the years and in 1980 I bumped into him at the Cannes Film Festival, where his latest film was in competition. He was not a happy camper.

"It's not fair," he said. "They have me competing today against your film "Being There" which cost several million dollars, while my picture was made for just one million. How can I win against those odds?"

I didn't see what difference the day of the screenings made and, above

OF KINGS AND QUEENS AND MOVIE STARS   179

all, I couldn't understand why the production cost of a film should be a factor.

"Bertrand, c'est l'art qui conte, pas l'argent," I told him. "It is the art that counts, not the money." In French this is a neat play on words as the words for art and money sound the same and I was rather proud of myself. Tavernier had no appreciation for my clever pun and continued to grumble.

Neither film won an award.

***

It used to be that all Hollywood producers seemed to be overweight, middle-aged men with loud voice and fat cigars. Nowadays, a producer is just as likely to be in his or her twenties and wearing shorts and sneakers. The cigar has been replaced by the cellular phone.

Back in 1961 we were still into fat men with fat cigars. The first of these specimens I met was Joseph E. Levine, king of the schlock. I had arranged an interview in his suite at the Dorchester Hotel with Tom Wiseman, show business writer for the London Evening Standard.

Levine was talking about "Sodom and Gomorra," a film which was still only in script stage.

"This is the biggest goddam epic that's ever been made," he expounded. "We got everything in it. There's earthquakes, there's volcanoes, there's flooding, huge battle scenes, tens of thousands of extras, everything!"

Wiseman put his head to one side, licked his pen and said quietly," Mr. Levine I'm not much of a Bible reader, but I don't recall all those events you just described as being part of the Sodom and Gomorra story."

Levine looked at his assistant seated in a corner. "Hey, Irving! You read the script. We got all those things, volcanoes, earthquakes and floods, don't we?"

"We sure do, Joe."

"There, you see!" said Levine triumphantly. "I told you it was going to be a great movie. We've improved on the Bible."

"Sodom and Gomorra" was eventually made, but by then Joseph Levine was no longer involved.

***

By definition, my job, obviously, is to publicize motion pictures. Sometimes, however, that job is to keep quiet and dam up any potential leaks. One such instance was "World Without Sun", a documentary made by famed underwater explorer, Jacques Cousteau. The expedition which Cousteau was working on was partially funded by the French government, which believed the film was to be shown only on state run French television.

If the bureaucrats learned that an American studio was involved and planned to release the film theatrically round the world, they could well withdraw their funding. The Gaullist regime of the time was particularly anti-American.

So it was that not a word about this underwater drama leaked out until production was finished and there was nothing the French government could do except stamp its collective feet in anger. "World Without Sun" won the Academy Award for best documentary in 1966.

***

Joan Chen, the beautiful Chinese actress who played the Empress in "The Last Emperor," used to have long, thick, black hair that reached almost to her waist. It had not been cut since she was 12. It was her pride and the joy of all who beheld her.

We soon put a stop to that!

She was about to shoot an action movie in Australia in which she had most of the action. Long hair wasn't right for the role. So I took Joan to a hairdresser on Robertson Boulevard in Los Angeles for the big lop.

Joan was very brave about the ordeal, shrieking only mildly when her long, shorn tresses were held up for inspection. Her new hairdo was no more than an inch long and she even grew to like it.

***

I was dining at the Lido de Paris club in Paris with George Segal and his wife. My date for the evening was Senta Berger. George was in town to promote the 1965 release of "King Rat." Halfway through the meal a waiter brought over a bottle of champagne with the compliments of "that gentleman over there."

We looked over and Jerry Lewis was holding up a glass in a toast and smiling at us. I'd never met him before, so went over to thank him and introduce myself as being from Columbia Pictures. We took an immediate liking for each other. Within a month, after 20 years of making films for Paramount Jerry signed a deal with us at Columbia. Well, yes. of course it was a coincidence.

***

Hervé Villechaise, the 3ft 11in "Tatoo" on the "Fantasy Island" television series, was a man who lived in fear of his life. I met him on the set of "Two Moon Junction" in which he portrayed a brutal carnival owner, a very different kind of role for him.

Hervé, who was born in Toulon, France, had a hard life. He quit school at the age of 11 to become a painter and was exhibiting his work by the time he was 16, emigrating to New York as a young man. He was dirt poor, making do on a few cents a day. He managed to sell a few paintings here and there. Unable to speak a word of English, he learned the language by watching television. Acting roles started to come his way and then his big break, "Fantasy Island."

He never forgot his own early tough life and worked with runaway kids in Los Angeles. He saw their young lives being ruined by drugs and told the police whenever he heard about a drug deal going down. He became a valued informer. Then word came that drug dealers had a contract out on him.

He showed me the gun he carried with him wherever he went, terrified that at any time a hired killer could be waiting for him. He told me there was much he wanted to do yet in his life.

On September 4, 1993 Hervé shot himself to death with the very gun he had shown me, despondent over his deteriorating health and not being able to find work.

***

Leo Jaffe, at that time vice-chairman of Columbia Pictures, didn't like to fly. So when he decided to go to the Cannes Film Festival he traveled by ship to Le Havre, taking a train to Paris' Gare du Nord. I was there to meet him and take him to the hotel where he would be staying for a few days before taking the train on to the Cote d'Azur.

He had a friend with him, a frail, elderly gentleman whom he introduced as Mr. Lloyd, explaining that he would be riding with us in the limo. We shook hands and I noticed that he had a couple of fingers missing, but gave it no further thought. The three of us talked animatedly in the car and I took an immediate liking to this Mr. Lloyd. He and Leo talked about the old days in films, but it was only when we were standing in the hotel lobby saying good-bye that I realized who he was. He was Harold Lloyd, the wonderful comic actor of silent movies. I remembered reading that he had lost those fingers doing one of his perilous stunts.

Harold Lloyd died a few years later. I was glad to have met this giant from the industry's earliest days.

***

I worked briefly on the production of "True Romance", which was released in the fall of 1993, bringing international press on to the set to interview the film's many stars, including Patricia Arquette, Christian Slater, Brad Pitt and Gary Oldman, and the director, Tony Scott.

On this particular day we were shooting a sequence in the historic Ambassador Hotel on Wilshire Boulevard in Los Angeles. The hotel had closed down a few years earlier and was now an abandoned hulk.

Ignoring "Keep Out" signs, I went exploring. What a strange sensation it was. Here was the famed Cocoanut Grove, at one time the most famous nightclub in all of Hollywoodland. There was the vast upstairs lobby, its dated leather armchairs still in place. I walked down a corridor of empty and abandoned shops, only the brand names etched on windows to remind me of more elegant days.

Idly I pushed open a swinging door and found myself in the hotel kitchen. I gasped, for I recognized the place. I walked to a spot in the middle of the room, alongside a long steel worktable and stood looking down at the floor. The place had been seared into my mind for 24 years, though I had never been there before. This was the site of Robert Kennedy's assassination by Sirhan Sirhan.

I stood silently, memories welling up. It was a strange and disturbing moment.

I returned to the present and to the scene that was being prepared at the rear of the hotel. Ironically, it was a gunfight.

***

Not all films a publicist works on are epics, or even feature length flics. In 2006 Murray Weissman and I helped steer a little 12-minute film to an Oscar® win. We ran the Academy Award® campaign for Ari Sandel's "West Bank Story," which was named Best Live Action Short in the February 2007 Oscar® ceremonies. A grateful Ari came to our office a few days later to show us his very special statuette.

***

FINAL WORDS

My first experience with movies was not particularly propitious. At the age of four I was taken to see "Snow White and the Seven Dwarfs," Disney's first full length animated feature. I came out of that cinema with a blazing headache and remember lying in a darkened room at home with a wet cloth on my head feeling very sorry for myself. It could only get better from there and it did. That four-year-old could never have imagined what movies would become and what importance they would play in his life.

Now maybe there'll be no more reason to travel round the world with those annoying, egocentric—and fascinating—celebrities. The global media can ask their questions via tele-conferencing while the star need not even get out of bed. Fans can already ask their questions and get answers via the Internet. Gossip magazine and television shows will no longer be needed and we certainly won't require globe-trotting publicists.

That would be a shame. I'd miss the Carlton Terrace in Cannes, the Bayerische Hof bar in Munich and that special, secret bistro on a side street in Paris. Most of all, I'd miss the friends I've made along the way.

Whatever happens, my personal happiness is assured. After a life of sometimes vicarious pleasures, of passing relationships and of loves lost, I have finally made the true connection.

Back in 1988, my cousin Alma flew into Los Angeles from her home in New York. I had known Alma off and on since I was four, when she lived in London with her mother. I had never met her two children and was only vaguely aware that they existed. On this particular warm summer's day she arrived with her daughter Elena-Beth, an actress, storyteller and computer consultant, who was then 30. I was immediately attracted to this beautiful, intelligent young woman with the warmest smile I'd ever seen. And just as immediately, I slapped myself on my mental wrist for entertaining such thoughts. After all, she was my second cousin and 25 years younger than me. Shame on me!

I invited them to my home for dinner and couldn't resist the temptation to show off my cooking, my oil painting and the liquor cabinet I had recently built from scratch. I was trying to impress Elena and at the same time keep my distance. Alma had to return to New York after a few days, but I persuaded Elena to stay on for a day or so and move from her hotel to my apartment. That night I lay in bed fantasizing that she would come into my room and into my bed. Of course, it never happened and I was angry with myself for even thinking the thought.

When Elena left, I took her to the airport. She wanted to hug me goodbye, but I was afraid to get close, pushed her away and gave her a quick peck on the cheek.

Over the following months and years, we wrote sporadically and spoke on the phone from time to time. In the fall of 1991 Elena called to ask if she could come stay with me for a week over Thanksgiving, staying a second week with our elderly cousin, Shelly, who lived in another section of Los Angeles. Of course, I said. It would be a wonderful celebration five times over. During Thanksgiving week my twin sons (who were living with me at the time) had their birthday. Three days later Elena celebrated her birthday and the very next day was my birthday.

She arrived and again I was struck by her beauty and grace. This time I felt vibes coming from her, directed at me. Again I lay in bed too chicken to make any approaches. After the second night I was sure that I had imagined those vibes. Nothing was going to come of this. She was my young cousin and that was all.

On the third evening I accepted an invitation from friends who owned the restaurant L.A. Farm, which had just opened. Joining our party were my colleague Michael Dalling, his ex-wife, Liz Dalling, who is a successful commercial agent, the actor Walter Gotell and a young actress/singer who insisted on engaging me in conversation the entire evening in the mistaken belief that I could help her career. Unbeknownst to me, Elena was deeply upset. She confided in Liz that she was drawn to me but I had shown no interest in her. Obviously I was more interested in the girl sitting the other side of me.

"Tell him," Liz said. "Men are stupid. They can't see what's under their noses."

"I'm sure he knows, he must know."

"Men are stupid!" repeated Liz. And then, in a tone that brooked no argument, "Tell him!"

As Elena and I drove home I was totally unaware of how she was feeling and what had been said. Men are stupid. We arrived at my apartment in Tarzana and, after I had checked my phone messages, she mumbled something.

I asked her to repeat what she had said.

"No! You're not going to make me say it again!" she moaned.

"I didn't hear you, honestly. What did you say?"

She swallowed, and looked straight into my eyes. "I said that for the last three days I haven't been able to stop thinking about kissing you."

My heart leaped. This woman had more guts than I did. After all this time my fantasy was coming true and true love was staring into my face. I stared back at her and forgot the passage of time.

As our lips touched I experienced something that I thought occurred only in those very movies I had publicized all my life. It was certainly nothing that could ever happen to this well worn, much traveled, old cynic. What I felt was a blaze of love, with fireworks exploding, trumpets blaring, the lot. The image that flashed into my mind was indeed like a scene from an old movie. You know the one. You're at the entrance to a magnificent golden palace. Servants open two huge doors and you enter a large chamber. At the far end are more double doors, another chamber, more massive doors beyond and so on. All this I saw in an instant. Each door opened showed more of our future. I saw us loving, living together, getting married, happy relatives and a future that stretched beyond time itself. All that in an instant.

Several days later Elena had to return to New York. We talked at length on the phone every evening for four months. After that we didn't need the phone. I met her at the airport with a limo, roses and champagne and she moved in. She must have wondered if she'd done the right thing, because a few days later we had the riots, then came the firestorms, floods and, of course, later, the Big Earthquake.

Elena was my personal earthquake, for she had truly turned my life upside down. I wanted to make her birthday that year a day she would never forget and took her to Le Dôme. I had it all worked out. I would

OF KINGS AND QUEENS AND MOVIE STARS

propose to her after we'd had dessert, but I couldn't wait and blurted it out over salad. In the wee hours of the morning, by which time it was my birthday, she woke me to say "yes".

We were married a year later, on the anniversary of that first kiss, at a place called The Storyteller Café. Elena designed the ceremony, which was as original as she is. Our honeymoon in Mexico was romantic and beautiful and unmarred by the unexpected.

Who'd have thought, with all my adventures and romances round the world, my hobnobbing with stars and royalty, that the love of my life would turn out to be my own second cousin. I know I lucked out.

www.ingramcontent.com/pod-product-compliance
Lightning Source LLC
Chambersburg PA
CBHW071700090426
42738CB00009B/1605